John Stott &
The Hookses

First published 2017 by

www.wordsbydesign.co.uk

ISBN: 978-1-909075-54-2

Further copies of this book, as well as details of other publications and services, are available from

www.wordsbydesign.co.uk

Picture acknowledgements:

The majority of the photographs have been taken by JRWS or David Cranston.

Thanks to Gordon Johnson for the photograph of his father Douglas Johnson on p.6.

Thanks to Mike Beale for the photograph of the Orion constellation on p.45.

All reasonable attempts have been made to identify the rights to all other photographs. Please contact the publisher with any queries concerning use of images.

Cover illustrations by David Cranston.

David Cranston completed his medical training in Bristol and worked in Exeter and Bath before coming to Oxford for post-graduate doctoral research. He is a Fellow of the Royal College of Surgeons of England and is currently Consultant Urological Surgeon in the Oxford University Hospitals NHS Trust, Associate Professor of Surgery in the Nuffield Department of Surgical Science and a Fellow of Green Templeton College, Oxford. Outside medicine he serves as a licensed lay minister in the Church of England and is on the board of the Oxford Centre for Mission Studies.

John Stott &
The Hookses

David Cranston

Dedication

For Rosie and in memory of her parents and my parents-in-law, Dick and Rosemary Bird,
"Who," in the words of John Stott in the introduction to his book *I Believe in Preaching*,
"for many years have accompanied me to my Welsh cottage, the Hookses,
and have unselfishly created the conditions in which I could write in peace and without distraction."

CONTENTS

Like many others, our first arrival at The Hookses after driving from Hertfordshire was in the gathering dusk. We took a wrong turn in Dale, realised that a gate into a cattle field was not what we were looking for, found our way to the single track around the back of the castle, trundled gingerly and disbelievingly past the indignant sheep along that airfield runway until, at last, we found the steep little driveway down to the welcoming lights of the buildings below (and a gratefully received sherry from Frances Whitehead). That was in September 2000, about a year before I was already expected to take up the reins of leadership within the ministries of Langham Partnership from John Stott. Part of the initiation process, it seemed, was an obligatory visit to The Hookses, which I had heard others talk about but had never been among the privileged visitors of the past half century, as mentioned in the pages of this book (and recorded in the much worn pages of successive visitors' books). So it was that my wife Liz and I were invited to join John and Frances, along with his then study assistant, Corey Widmer, and Rosemary

Bird, for a weekend at the sacred spot. A mere weekend, but it included some of the traditional rites – the communal washing up, the after-dinner reading and conversation in the tiny old lounge (this was before the major extension and refurbishing of 2004 and after), afternoon tea on the little patio outside the kitchen, and sherry after church on Sunday.

Like many others also, I marvelled at the simplicity of John's living arrangements in the Hermitage, and was ushered by Frances into the inner sanctum of his writing study for a conversation about my new role and the future of Langham. I could see his desk (that lovely old solid wooden structure that is still there and which I now regularly use myself) covered with the books and notes of his current writing project, and I knew that most of the Stott books written since the late 1950s had come to birth in this little triangular room gazing out to the sea, with Frances waiting in the room next door to commit John's small neat handwriting to typescript for the publishers. The sense of a hallowed heritage and an astonishing global influence

from all those books now being read around the world – all emanating from this small space – was overwhelming, while the presence of John himself in his very casual and (to be honest) threadbare Hookses attire was humble ordinariness embodied.

I still recall the slight hesitancy, almost anxiety, in John's voice when he asked me if I thought I might possibly consider using The Hookses as a place to do my own writing in future years (part of the deal with Langham, at John's insistence, was that my contract should include a commitment to give about three months throughout each year to writing ministry). He was relieved and delighted when I said, very heartily, that nothing would give me greater joy, or a greater sense of privilege, than to be allowed to spend time at The Hookses each year doing the kind of reading, reflection and writing that he had done there for decades. So that was agreed upon without hesitation, and he promised to make it available to me as often as possible.

True to his word, he made arrangements to enable that to happen. Space (both in cupboards and in the diary) was made for myself and a limited one or two others within Langham whose ministry includes writing – such as Jonathan Lamb while he was Programme Director for Langham Preaching, and Mark Meynell, Regional Co-ordinator for Europe for Langham Preaching – to make use of his private apartment from time to time. When the place was refurbished, he even ensured that the bedroom was furnished with a double bed so that our wives could join us if we wished. Later, the old communal washroom was converted into a separate little ensuite study bedroom, specifically for one of us to use if John, Frances and the study assistant were also in residence. It is now known as 'The Langham Den' (they considered my suggestion, 'The Langham Lodge' too grand), and several chapters of my books have been written in there when I shared occasional weeks with 'the happy triumvirate' as they called themselves.

After John's fall and hip fracture in 2006 and his move to the College of St Barnabas hospice in 2007, his visits to The Hookses became more difficult, given the length of the journey to get there and the challenging terrain of the property. So there was a deep poignancy when several of us shared a week there with him that we all knew would have to be his last. However, it would not be straying into any kind of sentimental or mystical realm (of which he would sternly disapprove) to say that his spirit lives on at The Hookses. So much of what still happens there now is what he desired for it. In the John Stott Flat and Frances Whitehead Office, which I still regularly use, many of the pictures and artefacts he gathered are still there, and I treasure, on the mantelpiece, a photo of us together, surrounded by nesting gannets, on a cliff edge in Newfoundland in 2003.

Above all, from a personal point of view, that initial conversation on our very first visit when he invited me to use The Hookses for my own writing, has gone on bearing fruit. For it is a fact that every book I have written since 2001 has had the benefit, at many stages, of weeks spent on various chapters down at The Hookses, and that will continue for as long as God enables. The place itself, the memory of the one who bought and enhanced it, the ethos of his lifetime of faithful writing ministry that was 'earthed' right there, the wild beauty of God's creation all around, the varied company of other friends from time to time in the main house, the sheer uncomplicated simplicity of days there (well, except when the boiler breaks down) – all these things continue to be an inspiration, privilege and joy, for which I am constantly grateful to our Father God, and our brother John.

Chris Wright
International Ministries Director
Langham Partnership

John Stott with Chris Wright

INTRODUCTION

DAVID CRANSTON

For those who have been there, The Hookses has always been a special place. It was described by one American visitor as, "A thin place", where the distinction between heaven and earth is very subtle. All who have visited, whether for longer or shorter periods, have come away with a profound sense of gratitude, not only for the fact that it was found and bought, but that the owner has been so generous in sharing it with so many people over the years. When a guest thought of comparing The Hookses to another place, John Stott would always say, "There is no other place like The Hookses."

On one occasion, flying back from the United States, as the plane started its descent to Heathrow, he looked out of the cabin window onto the Welsh coastline on a cloudless day and could see The Hookses several thousand feet below. It was a sight he always remembered and it brought great joy to his heart.

No one has been to The Hookses and returned unchanged, unrefreshed or unrenewed. It is a unique place, a haven for the weary and a rest for the soul. I hope this book paints a picture for those who have never been there, and refreshes the memory – if indeed it needs refreshing – for those who have stayed there. Now administered by the Langham Partnership and run by a small management group, it remains available primarily as a self-catering Christian retreat centre.

In 1951 John Stott travelled up to Glasgow to marry my parents-in-law, Dick and Rosemary Bird. They had known John from the late 1940s when they were members of All Souls Church in London. Rosemary worked as a nurse and Dick as a doctor and after their wedding they drove a Landrover and caravan along the North African coast to Jordan where they worked for the World Health Organisation until Dick contracted tuberculosis and they had to return. In London they ran the Medical Missionary Association hostel for medical students in Bedford Place and bought a family home in Inkpen, near Newbury in Berkshire, where John Stott would come to read and study for one or two days each year. Longer times were spent with him at The Hookses over many years.

Bishop Timothy Dudley-Smith, Prebendary John Collins and Frances Whitehead, along with my parents-in-law, appear on the first two pages of the original visitors' book at The Hookses in 1955. John Collins was with John Stott in 1952 when they first discovered The Hookses and he and his wife Diana were regular visitors thereafter. He was John's first curate at All Souls Church and was one of John's first residents in the Rectory at 12 Weymouth Street just north of the church, and has been kind enough to write down some of his early memories of those days. Frances Whitehead was John Stott's secretary for over 50 years and she and Timothy Dudley-Smith have been most helpful in their comments on this manuscript and his two poems are reproduced by permission.

The second chapter was written by John himself and has, to my knowledge, never been published. It was given by him to Jonathan Cranston when he was John's locum study assistant in 2002.

Many of the early photos in this books were reproduced from slides taken by John Stott in the 1950s and 1960s. Others were taken by the author or reproduced from photographs at The Hookses. The photo of the Orion constellation on page 45 was taken by Mike Beale.

Chris Wright has allowed me to publish his written reflections of the service he took in Dale Church when John Stott's ashes were buried in the cemetery there. I am also very grateful to him for writing the Foreword to this book.

Monty Barker was a consultant psychiatrist in Bristol and a close friend and mentor to me for 45 years. At the first Stott Bediako forum at the Oxford Centre for Mission Studies in Oxford in 2012, a year after John Stott's death, he wrote an appraisal of John Stott and his ministry, which forms the first chapter of this book. I thank the OCMS for allowing it to be republished here. I am grateful to Paul Bendor-Samuel, Executive Director of OCMS, and Michael Green for suggesting that this book should be written in the first place. Tony Gray has been very helpful and patient both as editor and publisher through his company WORDS BY DESIGN.

This is the story of John Stott
and The Hookses.

WHO WAS JOHN STOTT?

MONTY BARKER

Introduction

At the Memorial Service for John Stott in January 2012 at St Paul's Cathedral in central London, the words which seemed to me to sum up John Stott's life and ministry were those of a Jewish follower of Jesus, Mark Greene, the Director of the London Institute for Contemporary Christianity, when he declared:

> John Stott wrote for millions, preached to thousands, but invested in individuals.

In fact, few really knew him as a person. Many heard him preach but multitudes still read him as an author.

Who was John Stott?

I first came across John Stott's name in 1954. I was in a church in London, and came across a little book called *Men with a Message*. I began to read it, and the clarity, the depth and the breadth of this writer, of whom I had never heard, electrified me. I bought it for a shilling and kept it as one of those books which began my acquaintance with John Stott.

In the late 1950s I heard him as a student and listened to many of his talks. At one conference, John Stott and Martyn Lloyd-Jones were both speaking. Lloyd-Jones was the more charismatic preacher but I remember how carefully crafted John Stott's talks were. In the 1970s I shared a platform with John from time to time; I was the practical guy, but it was John who lifted the heart up to heaven.

I could never call myself a close friend, but his writing had a profound impact on me. Yet this man, who influenced the lives of millions, was never a Prebendary of St Paul's Cathedral as were his successors at All Souls Church; John Stott was never a member of the Church of England Synod; he was never a bishop, although he was an advisor to so many. In ecclesiastical terms, if you look at him at one level, he never 'made it.' Yet *Time* magazine named him as one of the most significant figures of the twentieth century, along with such people as Bill Gates. One of his contemporaries was David Edwards, a man with a formidable intellect who was on the liberal side of the Church of England. He was no fan of John's preaching or his

theology, but he said that, "apart from William Temple," a former Archbishop of Canterbury, John Stott was, "the most influential clergyman in the Church of England during the twentieth century."

Adrian Hastings, Professor of Theology at Leeds University, a historian of both the Church of England and global Christianity, said that John Stott, "must be counted one of the most influential Christian figures in the world."

John Stott would have seen himself primarily as an Anglican evangelical: Anglican because that was the church in which he was born and brought up and with which he wished to remain associated, but evangelical because this was integral to authentic Christianity. He said he was:

All Souls Langham Place

Sola scriptura sola gratia.
Under scripture and under grace.

Submission to scripture and submission at the foot of the Cross of Christ were at the heart of his life and ministry.

In a famous dialogue with David Edwards he said, "You see, the difference between us, David, can be summed up in the discussion between Luther and Erasmus. For, as Luther said to Erasmus, you sit above scripture and judge it, whereas I sit under scripture and let it judge me."

John Stott's Background

John Stott was born in 1921 in West Kensington and brought up in Harley Street, one of the most prestigious streets in London. At the age of eight he was sent away to boarding school. He then went on to Rugby, one of the leading schools of its kind in England and where the game of rugby originated. He was a prizewinner, a sportsman, and he became Head Boy. Rugby School was also where he became a Christian, at the age of 17 in 1938.

After leaving school he went to Cambridge University, where from 1940 to 1945 he was a student at Trinity College and then Ridley Hall. He was so disciplined that other people felt almost inhibited and wretched in comparison to him. A fellow student at that time said, "Everything he did related to Christ – it was so discouraging! But then we were able to have a good laugh with him and realised he was human after all!"

Even as a curate, John had an eye for the poor, for the outsider, and for the disadvantaged. He noticed the poor in the parish of All Souls, and he put the Clubhouse into operation for those who would never darken the door of the church.

In 1950 he became Rector, and he took his first major mission at Cambridge University in 1952. In 1970, he felt his ministry at All Souls should be shared with another person so that he could be freed for a wider ministry, and Michael Baughen joined as Vicar (later becoming Bishop of Chester) while John remained as Rector.

It was during these years that he began to think about other projects. These involved helping scholars from overseas to come for postgraduate research, and supplying literature at low cost to pastors around the world. So began the Langham scholarships and the Evangelical Literature Trust. He continued with his teaching ministry, his writing ministry, and his university missions throughout the world, and in 1974 he was Co-Chairman with Billy Graham of the first Lausanne Congress on World Evangelism.

He became Rector Emeritus of All Souls in 1975 and increased his global ministry, becoming Uncle John to so many people throughout the world. During this time he founded the London Institute for Contemporary Christianity with the aim of gathering together professional men and women and helping them to study together on how to live as Christians in every part of their lives, seven days a week, whether as a doctor or journalist or teacher or politician.

He was invested with a Lambeth doctorate, but had declined to be considered for bishoprics. In 1998, health issues forced him to give up driving and, in 2000, he asked Chris Wright to succeed him as Director of the Langham Trust which subsequently became the Langham Partnership International. In that year he was made a CBE (Commander of the British Empire) for services as chaplain to the Queen and his ministry to the global church.

In 2007 he moved to St Barnabas College in East Grinstead, a care home with a high Anglo-Catholic heritage. The care was outstanding, and he coped after a fashion with the prevailing tradition but he was not totally at home with it. That year he gave his last public sermon at the Keswick Convention. He asked to stand for it and managed to do so, holding on so tightly that his hands had to be prised away from the lectern, which was a sad but, in a way, a wonderful sight. He had no fear of dying, although he was perhaps slightly apprehensive of the process and certainly did not want doctors to strive officiously to keep him alive, for he knew that he had something wonderful waiting for him.

Framed above his bed in his room at St Barnabas College were the words of his life-long prayer:

> When telling Thy salvation free
> Let all absorbing thoughts of Thee
> My heart and soul embrace.
> And when all heads are bowed and
>   stirred
> Beneath the influence of Thy word
> Hide me beneath Thy Cross.

John Stott came from a privileged background, yet for 30 years he lived over a stable block in two rooms in Bridford Mews behind his previous Rectory. He could have made a lot of money from his books but lived frugally, using his money to forward the gospel and to found the Langham Trust. He was exceptionally gifted, but those gifts were not used to his own advantage but to the advantage of others whose gifts he could foster. He had a father who served in the First World War and was knighted for his services to medicine and to his country in the Second World War, but he chose to read Theology after obtaining a First in Modern Languages at Cambridge.

He did not live up to his father's expectations of him, not least in refusing the call to fight in the Second World War when he became a conscientious objector. Perhaps that was something of an adolescent rebellion, and John would say in his later years that he wished he had had someone to encourage a more reasoned approach at that time. His father would have liked him to go into the Diplomatic Service. However, he did take one thing from his father and that was a love of ornithology that remained to the end of his days. He often encouraged others to follow his love of birds, "For," as he said, "the Lord told us: consider the birds of the air and learn from them." He shared his love in one of his later books, *The Birds our Teachers*, and many people caught something of his passion and love for ornithology.

John Stott's Mentors

John Stott had a number of mentors. Eric Nash was his first. Eric Nash was employed by the Scripture Union and he had a burden for able young men coming from so-called public schools (which are actually private fee-paying schools) and wealthy backgrounds, who he felt could have a real influence if they became Christians. He ran camps for these people, and John Stott was one such. A friend commented about Nash that, "He showed John the loveliness of Christ, and John never lost sight of that vision." Nash did not just bring him to Christ: Nash wrote letters to him on a daily basis, when he left school, and later weekly, to encourage him and nurse him through his early days as a Christian.

Dr Douglas Johnson was another of his mentors. Known as DJ, he was the great strategist for evangelicalism. Not many people have heard of him, for he wanted to remain in the background. When Douglas Johnson was a medical student he arranged to be in three medical schools during the course of his studies, and while he was learning anatomy and pathology and physiology he would witness and talk about Christ. Christian Unions began in those three universities. He allowed students to make mistakes. He realised that if one tried to push them around,

Oliver Barclay

Douglas Johnson

they would rebel. DJ was probably one of the prime movers for the International Fellowship for Evangelical Students (IFES). When the possibility of bishoprics in Australia first came up, DJ was the one who said to John, "Be careful: I think you are of more value where you are now in All Souls than you would be in Australia. If I was the Archangel Gabriel in charge of heavenly postings, I would certainly keep you in Langham Place."

Oliver Barclay was a further influence on John Stott. Like Douglas Johnson he also preferred to remain quietly in the background, and is one of those unsung leaders of the church of whom few have heard. He was a brilliant man who, when he had finished his PhD, gave his life to the encouragement of students. He became General Secretary of what was then the Inter-Varsity Fellowship (IVF), now called the Universities and Colleges Christian Fellowship (UCCF). Oliver Barclay did not tell students what to do; rather he would say, "We need to have a chin wag," an upper-class way of saying, "Let's have a chat." He would take students for a walk and say, "There's another group doing so-and-so," which was his way of saying "I think you ought to think of doing this" – but he would never say it directly. Talking of John Stott, he said of their Cambridge days together, "There was one person who was such a wonderful witness that we could not put him on committees. His gifts would have been wasted spending time on committees."

It was Douglas Johnson who introduced John Stott to the historic ministry of Charles Simeon, and it was of Charles Simeon that John said, "He was something of a guru to me." Charles Simeon (1759-1836) was vicar of Holy Trinity Church, Cambridge for 54 years and his ministry was built on submission to everything that scripture taught, including those things that are difficult to reconcile. He said that the truth lies neither at one extreme nor the other, nor in a confused mixture of both, but in both extremes held together in tension, even if we may find that difficult to comprehend.

There were considerable similarities between Charles Simeon and John Stott. They were both bachelors, they lived in the same place for decades and they remained in the same church throughout their lives. They had a love for students and a ministry to them. They had a worldwide outlook: Charles Simeon was the one who helped found the Church Mission to the Jews and the Church Missionary Society, while having a deep social concern at the same time. Reading the biography of Charles Simeon helps one to understand something of the stable from which John Stott came.

John Stott's Legacy

Oliver Barclay said, "Something new was brought to life through the evangelism of John Stott. He was biblical; he was scholarly but not academic; he was firm but not caustic. He was a man with a more evident love for people than some of the old missioners and preachers."

The impact of his missions in the 1950s was probably greater than anything that had been seen since 1900. This was a new kind of evangelism, thoughtful and aware, yet not ignoring apologetics or theology. He could speak to the theology of others with sympathy as well as with biblical authority. His addresses at the university missions formed the framework of his book *Basic Christianity*, and brought many people into the kingdom of God in those years.

There were other events happening in Britain in the 1950s. Billy Graham first came to Harringay in 1954, and John Stott, among others, encouraged him when he was not sure if he could cope with England. His Crusade had a remarkable effect on the churches and theological colleges up and down the country. It also led to a friendship between Billy Graham and John Stott which resulted in the first Congress for World Evangelism in Lausanne in 1974, 20 years later. The

JRWS outside the Hermitage at The Hookses

friendship that had developed emboldened John Stott to withstand pressures from North America, and to give his support to those churches in developing countries which taught that evangelism must be associated with social engagement. The Langham Partnership grew out of this move towards holistic mission, and the Oxford Centre for Mission Studies also was deeply influenced by John Stott's understanding of this relationship.

Within the Church of England, John Stott revived the Eclectic Society that had been founded by John Newton in 1793. This was a group of young men in ministry who met to share fellowship together. Charles Simeon continued this and sometimes the men were encouraged to bring their wives, of whom he said: "In my ministers' meetings I also have the ministeresses, by far and away the better halves." There were echoes of Simeon when a Bishop said to me a few years ago, before the days of women vicars: "I invite the wives to accompany their husbands to clergy conferences; it earths them and they behave much better!"

John Stott's Writings

John Stott was a prolific author: fifty books came from his pen. He felt there was no greater need than that we should allow our minds to be conditioned and our lives reformed by the word of God. That was at the heart of his writing, but it was his preaching that led to his writing. Unlike some others, he did not just give a talk and then hand it to the printers. He would hone it, and it would go through his brain a second and a third time before he put pen to paper.

Issues facing Christians Today is, to my mind, one of his best books. He prepared what he thought the Bible said on different issues such as global poverty, ethnic diversity, ecology, sexuality, and the world of work. Then he would preach it to a group of representative people – in the latter case business tycoons, unemployed men, someone who was retired, someone who was redundant, as well as people in work. He would listen to their response and then re-write it, and finally it was published as a book. It is superb, bringing together scripture with issues in the modern world. He would listen to the word of God but would also listen to the parish, listen to

With Rob McKnight and John Yates at The Hookses, 1998

the press, listen to the journalists, listen to what else was going on. This idea of double listening came from Spurgeon, who used to speak of the need to have, "the Bible in one hand and the newspaper in the other."

The Bible Speaks Today series was a remarkable venture of which John was the New Testament editor. He began the series by writing on Galatians, and Martyn Lloyd-Jones said of this very lucid exposition that, "John told Paul what he should have written rather than what he actually said!" That is rather ungenerous, but nevertheless there may be an element of truth in it. Several contributors to the series said how John made very helpful editorial comments such as, "I think this might be better if it was put in this way," or, "Do you think it would be more helpful if..." rather than, "You should write this...." John himself contributed a further six titles.

He introduced the whole series by saying, "These expositions have a three-fold aim: to expound the biblical text, to relate it to contemporary life, and to be readable. There is nothing more necessary for the life, growth and health of the churches than that they should hear and read what the Spirit is saying to them through the ancient text."

A Buzzard outside JRWS's study

9

Bishop Holloway of Edinburgh was asked by the *Church Times* to review John's exposition of the Sermon on the Mount, *Christian Counter Culture*, and he said, as he read it on the train going from London to Edinburgh:

There I was on a high speed retreat led by John Stott and, like a lot of contemporary writers on the Bible, John Stott's intention is to let the Bible speak to us and to confront us by the Sermon on the Mount in a fresh and personal way without shirking critical issues. In this he has succeeded admirably. Reading the book was a salutary shock to me because, like many people who like to be thought progressive and up to date, I have been a little soft-centred when it comes to dealing with personal morality, though less so in the area of institutional morality. I need to be acquainted with the absolute standard of the holiness of Christ in private as well as in public behaviour.

Again, in referring to the discussion with David Edwards, it was Holloway who said in the *Church Times*: "David Edwards wants to make us think. John Stott wants to make us holy. We need to hear both challenges but

JRWS feeding white doves

John Stott's is the primary one."

John Stott gave himself to others. He loved people. He wrote letters to them in handwriting that was always legible. The letters were often short, always to the point, and elegant. Many Christian leaders have spoken or written of what John Stott meant to them, and often it was in his writing and in remembering things about them, in words of comfort and encouragement, sometimes in a closing prayer, sometimes in a passing comment, a balm to the soul. One scholar,

dilatory in finishing his PhD, received from John a most gracious but compelling jolt telling him to, "Get on with it!"

John gave himself in varying degrees to so many, but when it came to asking things of others and sharing himself with others it was only with a few. He sometimes had feet of clay, but that gives one the feeling that if God could use him maybe he can use me too. He knew what it was to suffer, to struggle and to have doubts. He did have outbursts of impatience and one saw this sometimes when

Bewick Swan over the Gann Estuary

he was tired: a flash of impatience, a quick answer to a question that was not so much an answer as a put down. And he had a rigidity that could seem ungracious at times. But like Caleb at 85 and even beyond the age of 85, his mind was active and he had no wish to be discounted because of his age.

Yes, there was a distance in him sometimes, a formality. He seldom spoke about singleness, or sex or dependency or loneliness, or indeed about his last five years in a nursing home with outstanding care but a high church tradition with which he was not particularly comfortable.

His last four books were more personal. In *Calling Christian Leaders* he attacks the culture including his own culture. In *The Living Church* he speaks of the need to love one's congregation. In *The Radical Disciple* he admitted weeping over his own dependency. In his Keswick address, *The Last Word*, there is a section where he speaks of the renunciations of his life: marriage, academia, and hierarchy, and yet in all those renunciations God richly rewarded him with other things.

It was Africans and his friends in Latin America who were best at breaking through his reserve. He loved Africans. They did not allow him to remain British, imprisoned in a tie, jacket and collar. Their joy and their effervescence swept him along, perhaps even allowing his knees to bend a little and his arms to float a little in singing and worship.

He had his chosen friends, he had his faults and his struggles – but what was it that really made him tick? It was his love for Christ, his desire to be like him, and his aim to share him with others, and like his mentor Charles Simeon, he resolved throughout his life and ministry to know nothing except Jesus Christ and him crucified.

Early Hookses, 1950

Years later, JRWS laying concrete

How the Author Became a Bird-Watcher, a Christian and a Landowner

John Stott

How is it that a town boy, a lifelong Londoner, born in West Kensington and brought up in Harley Street, came to travel the world and become addicted to the observation of wildlife in general and birds in particular?

My father was a physician, a specialist in heart and chests to be precise, who like any scientist took an interest in all branches of natural history. He was a keen amateur botanist, and I can still picture him clearly, with a monocular magnifying glass squeezed into one eye, minutely examining a flower's petals and sepals, stamen and pistil, and other anatomical details, in order to determine its identity. During the summer holidays, when as a family we escaped from London into the countryside, he would take me out for nature walks, telling me to shut my mouth and open my eyes and ears. It was excellent training in observation.

My first love was *Lepidoptera*, both butterflies and moths. Somehow, although I was only about eight years old, I was allowed to go out on my own, armed with butterfly net and cyanide bottle. Once caught in the net and transferred to the bottle, the captive butterfly would not survive for more than a few seconds. Gradually I accumulated quite a respectable collection, including a number of commas (which were regarded as quite rare until there was an invasion of them from the continent in the late nineteen twenties), and several species of fritillary – gorgeous combinations of brown, black and silver.

Although moths took second place in my affections, being largely nocturnal and less colourful, I was especially proud to have several specimens of the more unusual hawk moths. And one of the excitements of boyhood summer holidays was the adventure called 'sugaring'. During the day one concocted a lethal brew, consisting basically of beer, sweetened and thickened with black molasses. Then at sundown one went out into the garden or orchard and used a paintbrush

Painted lady

to smear each tree with a broad band of the beery treacle. The next step was to go to bed, and if possible to sleep, although excitement and expectation were not conducive to this. One was awakened at about midnight, and a little party of us would find our way back to the trees by torch light. Attracted by the sweet smell of the treacle, moths would drink their fill, become intoxicated with the beer, drop 'drunk and incapable' at the foot of the tree, and offer no resistance as we picked them up. My collection grew considerably by this dubious method.

Then one day disaster struck. I was setting butterflies for display when my sister Joy (13 months older than I, although often mistaken for my twin), provoked by something I had said, threw a cushion at me which landed plum in the middle of my butterfly box. If I have ever seen red in my life, I saw it then. My precious collection was ruined. Although my father tried patiently to stick the exhibits together with glue, they were beyond repair, and for days I was utterly disconsolate.

Looking back, however, this incident seems to illustrate the providence of God. I lacked the heart to begin assembling a butterfly collection all over again so I turned to birds instead. And now, I must confess, I am thankful to be a bird-watcher rather than a butterfly collector. On my travels, people sometimes look at me with quizzical amusement when they see me festooned with binoculars and camera gear; but what would their reaction have been if instead I were equipped with a butterfly net and a cyanide bottle?

Apart from my father, several boyhood friends encouraged me in bird watching. One was Robbie Bickersteth, a master at Oakley Hall, the preparatory school I attended outside Cirencester in Gloucestershire. Recently down from Cambridge, he was a man of great enthusiasms. He taught me to watch for the arrival of the first warblers on spring migration. He also helped me to construct a ramshackle hessian hide in the middle of a huge bed of nettles, so that I could photograph a nesting pair of whitethroats. I won the school photographic competition one year with a picture of a whitethroat perched on the edge of its nest. In the holidays, Robbie took me to the Norfolk Breck to see stone curlews and crossbills; to Scolt Head, an island off the north Norfolk coast, to photograph ringed plovers and terns; and to the Western Isles of Scotland in search of divers, which Americans call 'loons.' And he gave me the two volumes of TA Coward's *British Birds*, which I still treasure. Alas! Robbie was killed in Normandy after the allied landing in 1944.

My other boyhood birding friend was Alfred Stansfeld. Although he was older than I, and already at Cambridge while I was still at Rugby School, we had some great expeditions together. His widowed mother, 'Stanny' to her many friends and admirers, was headmistress of Centrecliff School in Southwold, Suffolk. Long before Minsmere became an RSPB reserve, that whole area was rich in waterfowl and shore birds. Alfred and I waded up to our waist in Walberswick Marshes in order to watch bearded tits, those comic little acrobats of the reed beds, and to

Baby curlew

follow the weird, resonant booming of the bitterns, until suddenly one would fly, its long green legs dangling behind. Alfred went into medicine, and in due course became head of the histology (morbid anatomy) department of St Bartholomew's Hospital.

Birding takes your mind off everything. It rescues you from the noise, the bustle and the pressures of city life, and transplants you into the tranquility of the wilderness. Few experiences are more healing to the spirit than rising with the sun and wandering out into the jungle, the African bush or an Asian paddyfield, if possible with a friend, but otherwise alone with the sights, the sounds and the smells of nature, and with the living God, who conceived and contrived it all.

I am able to say this only because of something which happened to me in 1938. I was at Rugby, approaching my 17th birthday, and restlessly seeking the reality of God. One Sunday afternoon a visiting clergyman spoke at the Christian Union meeting on Pilate's question: "What shall I do then with Jesus, who is called Christ?" I learned for the first time that some action on my part was necessary; that Jesus Christ was standing and knocking at the door of my heart and life; and that I had to invite him in as my Saviour and Lord. That night I opened the door to Christ. I saw no

lightning, heard no thunder, felt no electric shock. But gradually, as the days passed into weeks and the weeks into months, I knew that something radical had happened to me. And one of the evidences of my new birth was a new appreciation of the beauties of creation which, as I have discovered from my subsequent reading, is not an uncommon experience.

After I was ordained in 1945, I served my curacy at All Souls Church, Langham Place, next to Broadcasting House in the heart of London's West End. Not a very promising place for birds, you would think. But wait! The church had suffered bomb damage in December 1940. The bomb, which destroyed the Queen's Hall nearby, badly shook the church. The ceiling of the nave fell in and, in order to be rendered safe, the steeple had to be truncated. The Queen's Hall site was walled up and left derelict. All intruders were kept out – except black redstarts!

This dapper little fellow, all black but for a white wing patch and its flickering rust-coloured tail, was common in central Europe but had been regarded as a great rarity in England. It was recorded several times on the South Coast in the early twenties; but its first confirmed breeding site (wise little bird that it is) was in Cambridge – not in a college, however, but on a ledge of Eden Lilley's

furniture shop in 1936, 1937 and 1938. It was entirely appropriate, therefore, that the Cambridge University Bird Club should adopt the black redstart as its emblem. Then came the war. The holes in the walls of London's devastated buildings offered ideal nesting places to black redstarts, and they greatly increased in numbers. A pair nested annually in the Queen's Hall bombed site.

Often during 8 o'clock Communion on a Sunday morning in All Souls, when there was no roar of midweek traffic, I could hear a black redstart perched high up on the roof of the church or the BBC, singing its rasping, scolding, spluttering song, like the rattle of a handful of small stones. And there are other ways to watch birds in London. I think, for example, of the Royal Parks, and of the reservoirs which form part of the city's water supply and which are rich in winter-visiting duck like smew and goosander. Yet it was the summer holidays which gave me my best birding opportunities. Kitted out with tent, pressure lamp and stove, and cooking utensils, I used to go camping with friends in some remote spot. In this way we visited different parts of Scotland, East Anglia, the South Coast and the West of England.

In 1952, however, the decision was made to explore south-west Wales. The map seemed to indicate that the village of Dale in Pembrokeshire was as far away as one could get from main roads and railway stations. So one day my friend and colleague John Collins and I set out on our seven-hour drive. It was dark when we arrived, and raining hard. There was no possibility of finding a suitable campsite that evening. Instead, a friendly local farmer allowed us to doss down in his barn. If I remember rightly, we found that we were sharing our accommodation with a colony of rats, which kept John awake for much of the night and almost persuaded him to return to London the following day. But we awoke to a glorious sunny Pembrokeshire morning and walked along the coastal footpath looking for a sheltered spot in which to pitch our tents. The only place we could find was a little valley running inland from the cliff edge, which was watered by a small stream, and in which were situated an unoccupied farmhouse and its derelict stone outbuildings. The map informed us that its name was 'Hook Vale.' We soon discovered, however, that nobody called it by this name. Instead, local people invariably referred to it as 'The Hook' or 'The Hookses.' The latter name stuck. The landowner was Colonel Hugh Lloyd-Philipps of Dale Castle, and he gave us permission to camp there.

During the following month a number of other friends joined me, and we all fell in love with the place. We drank from the stream, and (further downstream!) washed in it. Then every evening we drove across the disused wartime airfield behind the house to the village of Marloes, where Mr and Mrs David Morgan of Glen View served us a magnificent evening meal. My favourite spot at The Hookses was, and still is, a grassy south-facing ledge about six feet down from the cliff top. Perched here, I can neither see any buildings nor be seen by any passers-by. All around me is the great sweep of the ocean.

To the west is bird famous Skokholm Island, and beyond it an outcrop of granite called Grassholm, where 30,000 pairs of gannets nest, and behind which the sun sets in a blaze of glory. Here, in my special nook on the cliff, I spent many hours in August 1952. For three months later I was due to lead my first eight-day university mission at Cambridge, my alma mater. This awesome responsibility filled me with apprehension. I

Dale Castle

Early days at The Hookses

think I understood what the apostle Paul meant when he wrote that he approached Corinth, "in weakness and fear, and with much trembling" (1 Cor. 2: 3). But here on my secret cliff-ledge I sat and thought and prayed and prepared and, I believe, met with the living God, until my heart's fears were largely pacified. And during the subsequent 45 years and more I have frequently repaired to the same sanctuary to think my thoughts, dream my dreams and pray my prayers. When there, some of the psalms have seemed especially appropriate as, for example, "the sea is his, and he made it, and his hands formed the dry land" (Ps. 95: 5).

But I have not yet divulged to you how The Hookses became mine. It was in 1954, two years after my first visit, that it came on the market and I was unfortunate enough to be outbid by Peter Conder. He was warden of Skokholm Island from 1947-54 and needed somewhere to live in the winter. I confess to having been bitterly disappointed to lose The Hookses to him, but I concluded that God did not mean me to become a landowner. However, no sooner had Peter Conder purchased The Hookses than he was

Skokholm 1956

18

appointed Reserves Officer and later Director of the Royal Society for the Protection of Birds (RSPB), which necessitated his move to Sandy in Bedfordshire. It meant that I was able to buy The Hookses from him.

During the next few years, necessary repairs and improvements were carried out until the house became habitable again and the outbuildings were converted into living accommodation. In consequence, several thousands of people have been able to share with me the unique beauty and tranquility of The Hookses.

Between two outbuildings, situated at right angles to one another, there was a triangular patch of turf, and in 1960 I had it enclosed and roofed over to form a study-bedroom for my own use which has come to be known as 'the Hermitage'. Of its three walls, one is lined with books, a second is equipped with a stove surrounded by pictures and memorabilia, and the third consists almost entirely of a south-facing picture window. So when I sit at my desk I look out over West Dale Bay, beyond which is the open ocean. And because of the diverse habitats of sea, cliff, stream and meadow, I have seen nearly 80 species of birds from the Hermitage. It is wonderful to see fulmars flying by with their strangely stiff wing beat, and to watch gannets diving head first

into the water of the bay from perhaps as high as 100 feet. They are said to hit the water at 60mph, the impact being cushioned by special air sacs underneath their head skin. Buzzards, ravens, wheatears and rock pipits nest on the cliffs. And on migration I have seen rarities on the airfield, like a dotterel, which breeds on the top of the Cairngorms in Scotland, and even once a buff-breasted sandpiper, which is a North American Arctic breeder and which had evidently been blown off course.

But my favourite Pembrokeshire bird is the chough. Although it is the rarest British member of the crow family, I am lucky enough to see them virtually every day from the Hermitage window. Usually they are in family groups of five or six but in July or August, after the young have flown, several families will congregate and I have seen as many as 24 in a single flock.

First of all, one is struck by their plumage of jet black with bluish sheen, and scarlet bill

The Hookses in 1956

Fulmars

Buzzard nest, 1968

Female Wheatear, 1964

and legs. Next, their aeronautical skills are phenomenal. They soar buoyantly, floating up and down in the wind like yo-yos. Then, closing their wings, they tumble and even plummet down before catching an updraught and swooping up again. They perform in the most carefree and cavalier fashion, however strong the wind, all the time emitting their wild, high-pitched cry, 'chee-ow' or 'ky-aa'. Choughs are less at home on land, although they are very efficient in gathering their food. Standing with their body horizontal and their feet planted firmly apart, they use their head as a hammer and probe deeply into the turf in their quest for grubs, beetles, ants and earwigs.

Although choughs are to be found in the mountainous terrain of Central Europe, and

across Asia to the Himalayas, they are restricted in Britain to the west coasts of Scotland, Ireland and Wales. Formerly, however, they were much more widespread. They were certainly common around the cliffs of Kent, since the arms of Thomas Becket, the twelfth century Archbishop of Canterbury (which are now the arms of the City of Canterbury), depict under the familiar lion rampant three perky standing choughs.

Friends who have visited me at The Hookses have remarked on its remoteness, for it is about a mile from the nearest other human habitation. It was connected to the telephone only in 1996 and to mains electricity only in 1997. Looking through my Hermitage window, and surveying the panorama of cliff, sky and sea, and ever-

changing colours, friends have also enquired how I can manage to concentrate when working at my desk. I can only reply that I find the view more inspiring than distracting.

I never cease to thank God for his provision of The Hookses. Its discovery was a notable example of serendipity, 'the faculty of making fortunate discoveries by accident,' since I found what I was not looking for. Both the Hermitage and my cliff-ledge sanctuary have proved a unique refuge in which I have been able, without interruption, to read, to think, to pray and to write.

It is impossible to express my sense of gratitude to God for this providential gift. I sometimes say to myself that I'm the luckiest man on earth. The intoxicating Pembrokeshire air, the beauty of the seascape

Choughs

Dotterell

JRWS in his nook...

and landscape, the stillness and seclusion, and the rich variety of birdlife, together make a uniquely satisfying combination of blessings. My favourite nook is a turf ledge a few feet down from the top of a nearby cliff. Here, especially in the early evening, as the declining summer sun paints the sea silver and gold, I love to sit either alone or with a friend, to read, to think, to dream and to pray. It would be hard to imagine a greater contrast than between central London and coastal south-west Wales, yet each has its own fascination, and I enjoy them both to the full.

... and Jonathan Cranston in the same nook

The Hookses on the Pembrokeshire coastline

LITTLE ENGLAND BEYOND WALES

DAVID CRANSTON

To the west of England lies the country of Wales, and the most westerly county in Wales is Pembrokeshire which has long been divided between an English-speaking south, known as 'Little England beyond Wales', and a historically Welsh-speaking north, along a reasonably sharply-defined linguistic border. The village of Dale is one of the most westerly villages in Pembrokeshire, and above the village of Dale, on a flat plateau overlooking the Irish Sea, lies a disused World War II airfield. In its own little valley, just to the side of one of the old concrete taxi-ways now pock-marked and overgrown with tufts of grass, lies The Hookses.

Pembrokeshire

The county of Pembrokeshire was once a Marcher Borough, a term originally used in the Middle Ages to denote the marches between England and Wales in which Marcher Lords had specific rights, which to some extent were exercised independently of the English Crown. In modern usage, 'the Marches' is often used to describe those English counties which lie along the border with Wales, particularly Shropshire and Herefordshire, but it also includes areas along the south coast of Wales, including Pembrokeshire, which were controlled from the thirteenth century by the Norman de Vale family who lived in Dale Castle.

The Celtic Church was indigenous to Wales, and it was during the early part of the Celtic period that David, the Patron Saint of Wales, came into prominence. He was born about 520AD into a noble family in south-west Wales, and after his ordination he founded a number of churches and monasteries and settled in Mynyw (which is now called St David's), about 40 minutes' drive from The Hookses. Since the sixth century there has been a church on the site upon which St David's Cathedral now stands. For the past 1,500 years prayer and worship have been offered to God on a daily basis, and that continues even now.

The present cathedral is the fourth church to have been erected on the same site. The first was built by David himself, but it was burned down in 645AD. The second and third buildings, hiding like the first in the

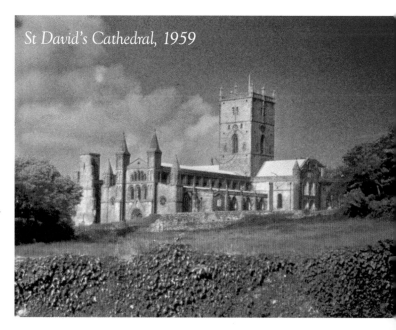

St David's Cathedral, 1959

Dale Airfield

Four razorbills, Skokholm

Young swallows in a nest at The Hookses, 1967

valley of the little Alun river, were built with a stunted tower designed to escape the notice of marauding Vikings, but it was nevertheless sacked by them in 1078 and 1088. The choir vestry in St David's Cathedral has a wooden plaque listing all the bishops of Saint David's going right back to David himself, and against five or six of them is written the one word, 'slain.' A number of western litanies at that time included the petition: 'From the fury of the Norseman, O Lord deliver us.'

The Pembrokeshire coast was forested in St David's day but he would have known the offshore islands that are familiar to visitors to The Hookses, as well as the wildlife on the mainland and in the coastal waters, and it was the little bay of Monk's Haven close to Dale that was thought to be the landing point for pilgrims travelling to St David's.

The county's coastline comprises internationally important seabird breeding sites and has numerous bays and sandy beaches. The cliffs and coastal path provide stunning views and the chance to see seals, dolphins, porpoises and even whales frolicking amongst the waves. It is also an excellent vantage point for seeing birds, with every season bringing different species into view.

Spring would see the arrival of swallows, warblers, and many of the seabirds such as Manx shearwaters and puffins, the latter first 'rafting' together offshore before heading to their burrows on the nearby islands.

Summer would herald the bustle and spectacle of the hectic breeding cycle of the seabird colonies, including razorbills and guillemots in their thousands lining the cliff tops and ledges around the islands. Everywhere buzzards, ravens and choughs – and less frequently peregrine falcons – could be seen, and over the last few years red kites have appeared over The Hookses. In autumn the Atlantic storms sometimes blow tired migrating birds off course, and the Pembrokeshire coastline provides them with a welcome respite.

Just off the coast lie the islands of Skomer and Skokholm, with Grassholm further away. John Stott and his friends often visited the closest two islands but occasionally made the longer trip to Grassholm, eight miles off the coast.

It was the Vikings who gave names to these islands, 'holm' being the Danish word for island. Gateholm lies at the far end of Marloes Sands and is accessible at low tide but becomes an island at high tide. Grassholm, the furthest of the islands, is owned by the Royal Society for the Protection of Birds. It is uninhabited by humans but home to more than 30,000 pairs of breeding gannets, eight percent of the world's population and the third largest gannet colony. Visible from the mainland it appears white in colour due to the vast amounts of guano deposited by the birds.

Skomer lies less than a mile off the coast and is the largest of the islands around Pembrokeshire. Skokholm is close by and easily visible from The Hookses, lying to the south of Skomer and a third its size. The name 'Skokholm' is Norse for 'wooded island', although today the island is very exposed as there are no trees (but willow, bramble and blackthorn scrub survive in the valleys). The narrow stretch of water between Skomer and the mainland is called Jack Sound, notorious for its strong tidal currents.

The isolation of these islands means there are no ground predators and for this reason they have become one of the world's most important breeding sites for puffins and Manx shearwaters, both of which nest in burrows. Some 165,000 pairs of Manx shearwaters breed on these islands, the largest and most important colony in the world. They spend their days fishing out at sea before returning to the island under cover of darkness to avoid any potential airborne predators. Although there are thousands of holes on the island, the birds come back to the correct one every day and often re-use the burrows year after year. Manx shearwaters may live for up to 50 years and, as they normally migrate to South America, may fly well over one million miles in their lifetime.

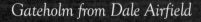

Gateholm from Dale Airfield

Kittiwake and chick, June 1967

Puffin, Skomer, 1968

They are not alone in their nocturnal activities: storm petrels also wait for the safety of darkness before returning to the islands where there are about 5,000 pairs, twenty percent of the European population.

In his book *People My Teachers* John wrote:

We cannot be sure that the breeding habits of local seabirds were the same in David's day as they are today but I guess they were not very different. We certainly marvelled today at the 30,000 pairs of gannets which occupy the whole of the north-west corner of Grassholm, and at the tens of thousands of puffins and Manx shearwaters which lay their single egg in the burrows under our feet on Skomer and Skokholm, and at the

fulmars, kittiwakes, guillemots and razorbills which occupied the perilous cliff edges at different levels.

Between the puffins, shearwaters and rabbits there are very few spots on the islands which have not been dug out, and just beneath the surface lies a honeycomb of intricate tunnels and burrows used for shelter, protection and nesting.

Dale

Dale remains an unspoilt village with a population of a few hundred in the heart of the Pembrokeshire Coast National Park. Situated 25 miles from St David's and 12 miles beyond Haverfordwest, it is located on the Dale peninsula which forms the

northern side of the entrance to Milford Haven estuary. It has been English-speaking since the twelfth century.

Dale is host to two significant buildings in its village, Dale Castle and Dale Fort, as well as the church. The Gann Estuary is nearby, and The Hookses is accessed through a disused airfield on the plateau above the village. Dale Castle was built by the de Vale family in the thirteenth century after the Norman invasion of South Wales. The history of the old castle is obscure but the de Vale family lived there between the thirteenth and fourteenth centuries, possibly giving the village its name, although it is more likely that the name came from the Vikings who settled there at one time, as the word 'Dalr' meaning 'valley' is Norse in origin.

Little remains of the original medieval castle. The present house and farm were remodelled in 1910, built in the style of a fortified manor house. Owned now by the Lloyd-Philipps family and their trusts, they have sold much of the remaining land, including the island of Skokholm which they once owned.

Dale Fort is a mid-nineteenth century coastal artillery fort sited on a rocky promontory at Dale Head and was completed by 1858. The fort was intended to protect the anchorage at the mouth of Milford Haven by providing interlocking gun placements with the nearby forts. It now houses a field centre for the study of local marine biology and other related fields.

Across the road from the castle is the church frequented by many visitors to The Hookses. It has a late medieval tower and outer walls which have a crude, grey roughcast cladding. Although there may have been an earlier religious settlement here, it is probable that the de Vale family established a church on its present site. The church is dedicated to St James the Great, one of the apostles, who is also the patron saint of pilgrims. The bell in the tower was probably added in the sixteenth century and may have been used as an aid to navigation for vessels approaching the harbour and anchorage of Dale. This was the church that John Stott usually attended when he was at The Hookses.

The churchyard had become too small by 1890 and a new cemetery was consecrated a little way to the south. Among its graves and memorials are several honouring those who died serving at local military bases or during the two World Wars, and it is there, at the rear of the cemetery with a view over the hills and the coast, that the ashes of John Stott were laid to rest in 2011 beneath an imposing black

Welsh slate gravestone. Chris Wright describes that service at the end of this book.

John Wesley visited Dale on Thursday, 22nd August 1771, which he calls 'Dala' in his journal, a little village at the mouth of Milford Haven. It is unclear whether he preached in the church or out of doors, but he recorded that:

...our preachers had bestowed here much pains to little purpose. The people, one and all, seemed as dead as stones, perfectly quiet and perfectly unconvinced. I told them just what I thought. It went as a sword to their hearts. They felt the truth and wept bitterly. I know not where we have found more of the presence of God. Shall we at last have fruit here also?

The Gann Estuary, where many of the afternoon bird-watching trips took place, is one of Wales' four coastal lagoons just outside Dale. A long shingle ridge separates the estuary from the Pickleridge Pools and this forms an unusual habitat for wildlife, for the

Pickleridge Pools

The Gann Estuary

large pools are fed throughout the year by freshwater streams but also flooded by the sea during higher tides. These pools are not natural features – they were created from the extraction of building materials needed for the nearby World War II RAF sites above Dale and at nearby Talbenny. The pools attract ducks and geese as well as wading birds and wildfowl which are enticed by the rich feeding grounds of the estuary. During the summer, shelduck, oystercatchers, snipe, redshank and green-shank are familiar sights, and in autumn whimbrel and hundreds of greenfinches and pipits visit the area. In winter large groups of curlew are often seen, along with little egrets with their dagger-like bill and brilliant white plumage, the latter a relative newcomer to the Pembrokeshire coast.

Dale Airfield sits on a flat plateau above the village. It was built as an RAF station in 1942 to combat the menace of the U-boats in the Second World War. Initially the station operated Wellington bombers of No. 304 (Polish) Squadron. They flew on anti-submarine patrols for convoy protection missions, but raids on enemy shipping were also carried out over the French coast as far south as Gironde Estuary on the Bay of Biscay. Returning to base on the exposed peninsula was a hazardous operation in bad

weather and, as well as the dangers experienced on these missions, crews suffered fatalities caused by the difficulties involved in landing or taking off from the exposed airfield.

One particularly tragic accident occurred on 11th August 1942 when a Wellington bomber was taking off on an anti-submarine sweep. The runway into wind was unserviceable, and the aircraft failed to get airborne in the strong cross-wind and went over the cliff into the sea. Despite all efforts at rescue, there were no survivors in the rough waters. In Marloes Church there is a Roll of Honour to those Polish aircrew and others who died serving at Dale.

A number of other types of aircraft operated from Dale, including Beauforts, Beaufighters and Mosquitoes, and one unofficial job which fell to the Dale squadrons was dropping supplies to the lighthouse keeper on Skokholm, flying as low as possible to throw packages out of the window, or drop crates through the torpedo doors.

In September 1943 Dale was passed to the Royal Navy, supporting the flight training carried out at Kete. It remained in this role until it closed in 1947. Five years later, when John Stott discovered The Hookses, the remains of all this activity was still clearly to

Oyster catcher and nest, Skokholm, 1959

be seen. Disused runways crisscrossed the former farmland. Grass was growing across the tarmac and some of the buildings were used as storage by a local farmer. The little farmhouse with its outbuildings in 'Hook Vale' was untenanted and falling into ruin.

Seventy years later the runways are still there and have provided driving practice for two generations of young visitors to The Hookses. Most of the airfield buildings have been demolished, but a skeleton of one hangar still stands, along with several workshops and accommodation buildings on private land to the north-west of the site. One of the huts contains paintings of aircraft and other 'barrack room art', and is a Grade II listed building that can still be visited.

Skokholm

THE HOOKSES

DAVID CRANSTON

The Hookses occupies a truly spectacular position within the Pembrokeshire Coast National Park. A 186-mile coastal path trail skirts the property just outside the boundary fence, while sheep graze peacefully across the airfield and along the cliff edge.

On entering Dale the driver proceeds around the one-way system to find a small single-track road opposite the church. Continuing up this to a farm gate the visitor comes across a notice reading, 'No entry without permission'. Hesitantly they go through the gate and find themselves on the taxi-way of the old airfield. There is no building in sight. Driving down 400 yards they then come to a sign which says, 'The Hookses', and down to the left, along a short length of tarmac road, there it sits, nestled in its own little valley, on the cliff edge with the vast expanse of the ocean beyond – an approach and a view that has changed little in the 65 years since John Stott first saw it in 1952.

The nearest land due south is Cornwall, south west the Azores, and due west the southern coast of Ireland. When looking past all three, John Stott would say he had an uninterrupted view to the South Pole! There are days of blue skies and glorious calm and others, especially during the autumn and winter storms, when the white breakers on the tops of the waves can be seen far out to sea and the wind funnels up the valley towards The Hookses, as the salt sea spray lashes against the windows of the house.

Chris Wright summed up the autumnal weather in his entry in the visitors' book in October 2000: "One day of horizontal rain followed by a day of glorious sunshine." Another visitor wrote: "Stood on the airfield in a wind of 107mph."

Snow is rarely seen at The Hookses due to its position on the coast, the Gulf Stream, and the salt spray blown up from the sea, although an entry in the visitors' book in December 1995 mentions a light touch of snow at The Hookses.

John Stott has described his discovery of The Hookses. John Collins was with him at that time and has his own memories of that trip. He writes:

John liked to keep surprises up his sleeve. In March 1952, less than a year after I had been in London, I received a warm little note from him: Would I spend a week of my summer's holiday with him? Included was a list of camping equipment required: a tent, a camp bed and so on. John's eye was on a remote line of coast north of Dale at the south-west tip of Wales, the haunt of sooty cormorants, sleepy seals, greedy gulls, and – to my mind the only really attractive seabirds – gannets diving at 60mph, and beautiful terns that I had watched and loved on the Cornish coast; yet I was uncertain – I like my creature comforts on holiday. My memory of tents in north France being blown away at 2.00am was a dissuasive, and I disliked swimming which I found a cold, slimy sport! On the other hand the opportunity of spending time with John appealed strongly and, in the end, won.

It was a long journey through serious rain. We rose at 6.00am, left 12 Weymouth Street at 7.00am, and

Buff-breasted sandpiper

Cormorant

reached Dale at 8.00pm. John's car was an ancient Dutch Army truck with the remains of plastic windows. A bumpy ride. I had a headache, the previous night being too short for me. John himself was unsympathetically cheerful. He suggested that we should climb the hill at Dale so that we could look over the sea. We arrived at the farm, and the farmer kindly said that we might spend the night in his barn. I remember looking out of the barn door at the dark grey sea; and above it the even darker grey sky, only broken by one streak of angry red sunset.

If I had travelled in my own car I might have turned around and gone back to London immediately. In retrospect, I am very glad that I did not. I would have disappointed John and left him in the lurch, and I might well have qualified for the discouraging title of a certain Prime Minister in the Middle East, of whom it was said that he never missed an opportunity of missing an opportunity.

John Stott suggests that I had a sleepless night due to the other occupants of the barn - a family of rats. But Welsh rats are better behaved than Nepali rats that fight all night and, despite rats and rain, I slept quite well, and to our surprise the next morning was the first day of a fortnight of glorious summer weather. The Hookses lies in a hollow, and is not visible from the barn where we were spending the night. We walked happily together along the coastal path, John keeping an eye on an untidy bag of feathers above us, a buzzard looking for its breakfast, until we reached a farmhouse with deserted outbuildings - The Hookses.

The breeze was gentle, but the buildings and the little recess in the clifftop in which they stood provided welcome shelter should we need it. So there we pitched our tents, and both of us chose a comfortable nook in the cliff looking out to sea, took out our books, and settled down to a read.

It was a good holiday. Both of us had brought a pile of serious books that we wanted to read. But we also planned to read to each other. So I also brought *Saki's Short Stories* by HH Munro, and – would you believe it? – John had brought his copy of Saki too!

I was glad to introduce him to Arthur Haslam, the amusing, cultured clergyman of Baldhu Church near Truro who was converted through one of his own sermons in 1831. A member of the congregation – sensing that the vicar was suddenly speaking with new authority and conviction as if he really believed what he was saying – was unable to contain his enthusiasm, shot up like a meerkat at the back of the church and shouted, "Parson's been converted!" Whereupon, this being Cornwall, all heaven was let loose. As we read both these books we often had to stop. Tears of laughter were running down our cheeks.

When John Stott and John Collins came across The Hookses in 1952, it was unoccupied and dilapidated, but in 1954 it was put up for sale for £1,000 with a notice stating that, "Being situated within the National Park, it would have great potential as a café"!

As John writes in chapter two, he made an offer on it but was outbid by Peter Conder, Warden of Skokholm. However, no sooner had he bought The Hookses for £800 than he was appointed Director of the Royal Society for the Protection of Birds and was required to move to Bedfordshire. So John Stott was able to buy it and paid £750, but then after meeting Peter Conder in London some months later, gave him another £50 as a goodwill gesture because he did not feel he could pay Peter less than he had paid for it.

John's early researches into the history of the property showed that it was probably built in 1847 as two cottages side by side. On 4th April 1848 James and Mary Davies were married and then lived at The Hookses, and they were probably its first occupants. A date of 1888 was burned into one of the beams, now hidden from view, of the barn which is now Meg's loft.

In 1891 a census recorded that 'Hooks Farm Dale' was occupied by Mr Lewis Williams, farmer, and his wife Mary, their step-daughter Eliza, a ploughboy aged 17 and a cowboy aged 13. There are no further records until 1937 and 1938 when the cottages were re-conditioned and extended during this year, and in 1942 during World War II the property was requisitioned by the Royal Air Force.

Gann Estuary, 1998

*Laying the garage foundation,
and building a wall with friends*

Soon after purchasing The Hookses, John Stott drove down to examine it. In December 1954 a severe storm had blown the roof off one of the lower buildings and landed 200 yards away on the airfield. Fortunately John was able to claim £90 storm damage on Peter Conder's insurance policy to have it re-roofed.

The Hookses was also eligible for a post-war improvement grant of £400, provided that certain conditions were met, including connection to mains water and installation of a septic tank. While this work was being done a Rayburn stove was also fitted for cooking and hot water. These improvements rendered the house habitable, and in early 1955 various friends were invited to stay to help decorate and make it more comfortable.

Twice a year John Stott would organise 'do-it-yourself' weeks at The Hookses when a number of close friends with appropriate skills would join him for maintenance and small building projects. He was competent at mixing concrete or helping to build walls, and equally happy on his knees smoothing out the concrete drive, digging the foundations for a new garage or in waders cleaning out the pond. But on one earlier occasion, before he bought The Hookses, he was involved in another intrepid episode, as John Collins recounts:

Late one morning in 1952, John and I were walking up Upper Regent Street towards All Souls Church. He was dressed in his black suit and dog collar, and a man as huge as GK Chesterton whom I thought, from his clothes, was a builder, crossed the road and said to him, "Are you, by any chance, the vicar of this church?" John said, "Yes I am, how can I help you?" "Well," the builder continued, "I am the senior steeplejack working on repairing the steeple. We are just about to screw on the top of the steeple; it is an iron point, and all you have to do is turn it to screw it on – it's quite simple. We wondered whether you would like to come up and do it?" John turned to me and said, "Shall we do it together?" So off we went....

The steeple of All Souls rises out of a drum, decorated on the outside with a colonnade of little Corinthian pillars to echo the great pillars round the portico. I would guess that this drum is about half-way up the tower. To reach the top of the drum was easy going. But then, only an all-too-flimsy ladder climbed up the side of the steeple until it reached a small wooden platform. In the centre of this platform the top of the stone steeple peeped out. From the bottom rung of the ladder, that glimpse of our goal seemed close to the sky! Indeed, in the words of the hymn it appeared to me to be like the 'home for little children above the bright blue sky.' I began to feel that things were taking a turn for the worse. Moreover, the steeple itself was fluted, so the ladder never rested quietly and comfortably. It wobbled from side to side.

"Don't worry, Sir," said the big steeplejack breezily, with a twinkle in his eye. "Hold on tight to the sides of the ladder and you will be quite safe. We will grasp you when you reach the top." He was absolutely right – we soon reached the top. Three tough steeplejacks grasped us and pulled us on to the little platform.

John bent down and quickly screwed on the point: a fine black-and-white photograph of John Stott, the young steeplejack, was taken with his hand twisting the sharp steeple point. Behind and well beneath him is the roof of the BBC building. Then came the descent. Not so easy! The senior steeplejack gave us exact directions. Nevertheless we had to begin by swinging our right leg away

Stripping wallpaper and fixing the crooked weather vane

Ready to work, and (earlier in his life) screwing on the top of the steeple at All Souls Church, 1952

from the platform over the abyss. I did not intend to look down, as my leg waved about in the air feeling for the top rung of the ladder. But one rash glance could scarcely be avoided. There were the taxis, a shadow of their normal size, disappearing down Queen Anne Street in the deep shade of the Langham Hotel, or like tiny insects racing up Portland Place and vanishing towards the Marylebone Road and the Royal College of Music. At that size, they seemed to me to be of more interest to a student of nanotechnology than to us marooned on our draughty little platform, but we returned safely to terra firma.

At The Hookses, all the major construction work was carried out by external firms but the majority of the other work was done by John Stott and his friends in the 'do-it-yourself' weeks.

Driving from the airfield, the main house is on the right set into the cliff face. The two chimneys on the main house almost reach the level of the surrounding airfield plateau. The house is a light shade of pink with a roof of black Welsh slates. An old ship's bell hangs to the side of the front door which is situated

Looking out across Helen's Hut and Jo's Barn in the 1970s

at the end of the house, out of the wind. Inside a stairway goes up to the right, leading to the two original double bedrooms, and on the cliff side of the house two additional single rooms have been added, one named Joy's Room, after John's sister who left a legacy to be used there; the other room was named after Joy's beagle, 'Fanny', who was described as "as bad in character as she was good in looks."

An extension to the main house was completed in 2004, and John Stott describes its dedication in his New Year letter of 2005:

The new extension was dedicated in September to the glory of God and the blessing of his people. Bishop Michael Baughen kindly came to the dedication. It was attended by about 60 people who braved strong winds and

The Hookses in 2017

heavy rain to be there. We were especially glad that about half of our guests were from the three local village churches of Dale, Marloes and St Bride's. We are extremely grateful to all our donors on both sides of the Atlantic for their help with the restoration. Special mention must be made of Martha Ashe, whose generous gift made possible the extension. The new lounge is named the Martha Ashe Room after her.

Hanging on the back wall of this room is a magnificent oil painting of a cliff seascape looking towards West Dale, painted by James Bartholomew (2006). Below the Martha Ashe Room is a new games room with darts, table tennis and snooker available for the entertainment of visitors.

Many different varieties of birds adorn the inside of The Hookses, including a dangling albatross over the dining table with a cord which when pulled makes the wings move up and down. John Stott would pull this every morning and mimic it with his arms in his early morning exercises as he came and stood by the breakfast table before Grace was said.

Below the main house and set into the cliff is the old barn, and at right angles to it is the Langham Den and a room used as an office where Frances would sit and type, with a small kitchenette at the rear. When The Hookses was bought, the floor of the barn loft was riddled with woodworm and replaced, and then the loft itself was partitioned into sleeping quarters for groups of young people who came down from All Souls Church. It was named Meg's Loft, after Margaret Allen, a nurse who died in 1998 leaving a legacy for its refurbishment. Below was initially a games room, later converted into larger sleeping quarters for John Stott, complete with a picture above his bed of a snowy owl perched on a rock.

The two buildings were connected in 1960 by a triangular extension costing £350 which became John Stott's study and this, together with the office and sleeping quarters, was then known as 'the Hermitage', with its stunning

Much-loved painting owned by
Sir Arnold Stott of a fly fisherman

view across West Dale Bay and out to Long Point and St Anne's lighthouse. Another much-loved picture which belonged to his father, Sir Arnold Stott, depicts a fly fisherman on a mountainous river, and hangs on the office wall.

Close to the Hermitage and behind the workshops is the 'Gorlan,' Welsh for sheepfold, formed as a natural enclosure hemmed in by the cliff on one side of the workshop and a low stone wall on the other two sides. The area is often used for barbeques in the summer.

To the left of the main house as one faces the sea, across the little stream that runs through the property, are Helen's Hut and Jo's Barn, accessible across a small bridge made of old railway sleepers. These were the stable and byre of the old farm, and in 1967 they were converted to provide one double and one single room, now both ensuite rooms for visitors. Helen's Hut is named after Helen Menzies who entertained hundreds of Christian students in her Welbeck Street London flat, and she left a small bequest which paid for the conversion. Jo's Barn is named after Miss Jonas, or 'Jo' to her friends, who died in 1961. She was another member of All Souls Church and a frequent visitor to The Hookses.

Painting of West Dale Bay, by James Bartholomew (2006)

Prebendary Dick Lucas recalls that on his early visits it became customary for him to take up residence in Helen's Hut which he was glad to do except in the night, when nature called. Then, well wrapped up against the wind, torch in hand, he would tread carefully across the two planks over the stream, then over the long wet grass in which legions of slugs conducted their amorous nightly exercises, finally to reach refuge in the men's washroom. Having heard that Helen's Hut is now ensuite he was gracious enough to congratulate his successors, even if he could not wholly approve of such self-indulgence.

In 1974 a fence was erected around the property, and the following year Calor Gas was installed which marked the end of oil lamps and candles. In 1982 the bottom of the stream was concreted from Helen's Hut to the waterfall, and the following year the fence was

Weeding a pond in 1992

Making a bonfire in 1997

creosoted, taking four volunteers five hours and 15 gallons of creosote.

On one occasion in 1983 during a 'do-it-yourself' week, stones were brought up from the stream to raise the height of one of the workshop walls, incorporating a couple of huge stones which John and a colleague lifted into place which remain there to this day. 1985 saw the garage assembled and erected, and the classic picture of John Stott in jeans with bucket in hand was taken during its construction (see page 34). The garage stood for 30 years until it blew down in 2006 in the worst storm that he could remember.

In April 1992 John Stott and three friends laid a concrete path 30 feet long outside Frances Whitehead's office so that she would

The garage after the storm of 2006!

not get her feet wet in winter. Having just celebrated the 36th anniversary of her becoming All Souls Church secretary, the path was renamed, 'The Frances Whitehead Walkway'!

The gas lighting continued for the next 22 years until 1997 when electricity was installed at a cost of £25,000. This involved major work in bringing cables across the airfield.

The Hookses has always been a place of peace and tranquility where people come apart to rest awhile, to worship and to pray. That was true for John Stott and remains so for all those who have been guests there, and his memory still surrounds and permeates the place.

Frances Whitehead always said that John came tired, worked very hard, and came away totally refreshed. When one is there, time seems to stand still, and the days pass but the names of the days blur into one another.

Sheltering the inhabitants from nature's onslaught for the last 60 years, The Hookses has been a place of physical and spiritual refuge, relaxation and restoration for those who are enduring the storms that life throws up.

Missionaries have come worn out and been refreshed and rejuvenated; ministers have come burnt out and gone away recharged and restored. To many it has been a port in the storm of life, where one leaves behind the stresses of everyday existence and discovers the presence of God in a fresh way; a stopping place where men and women are given pause to reflect and to wonder at God's creation and stand back from the mundane rituals, the grief, trials and boredom of day-to-day life. A place to love and to be loved; a place to find peace.

Entries in the visitors' books over the years testify to its restorative effect:

A beautiful place to take a step back from the chaos of normal life.

A perfect place to recharge batteries. We were so tired and tense on arrival – now relaxed in the enjoyment of Isaiah 35. A glimpse of heaven on earth.

We came hungry for rest and relaxation. We were looking for a place to escape the congregation. Thank you Hookses – this was exactly what we needed.

If such wonderful times can be experienced on earth, how lovely indeed must the dwelling place of the Lord be!

Perhaps the spiritual life at The Hookses is no better summed up than in the words of the hymn by David Evans:

Be still, for the power of the Lord
  is moving in this place:
He comes to cleanse and heal,
  to minister His grace.
No work too hard for Him,
In faith receive from Him.
Be still, for the power of the Lord
  is moving in this place.

Every season at The Hookses has its own special attraction. Spring sees lambs gambolling on the airfield and a host of golden daffodils fluttering and dancing beside the stream, and the valley fills with wildflowers. Yellow flag iris grow where the stream runs into a little pond beside the Hermitage. There are marsh marigolds, bulrushes, purple loosestrife and red campion flowering all summer in the damp places by the stream. In the pond itself the waterlilies open for the dawn and close at dusk, and marsh trefoil spreads matted root stocks out into the water.

One Spring John wrote:

It is wild and wet down here. Huge rollers are pounding on the rocks. Great globules of spume are being blown up into the valley. The stream is in spate. The new turf we laid is excellent. Despite the weather, white and purple heather are in full flower in the rockery, and the rowan tree has healthy buds on its lower branches.

Summer arrives with its outdoor barbeques and trips to Marloes Sands or West Dale Bay. In autumn the storms come whipping up along the valley, and the winter months also have their attraction, of which John wrote:

Even during the gales of midwinter The Hookses is safe and snug. It is well sheltered from the north-east and west. It is exposed only to the south. Then when southerly winds blow, the great Atlantic rollers pound against the cliff and drive the rain horizontally up the gully. Once or twice I have seen the whole valley white not with frost or snow but with spume. Then the following day the bracken has turned brown from the salt. Its powers of regeneration are amazing.

Red campion in Pembrokeshire

Retrieving a Manx shearwater from burrow, 1984

Picnic on Skomer with Mansell and Noreen Connick and Dick and Rosemary Bird, 1984

Reading Saki at The Hookses, 1984

With Chris Jones and Frances Whitehead, 2006

It would be a mistake to think that the views from The Hookses are spectacular by day only, for night views can also be amazing when the skies are clear. The black night sky is unadulterated by artificial lights and largely hidden from Dale. One entry in the visitors' books reads:

The milky way and stars were amazing. I have never seen such a lovely and clear night sky.

The prominent constellation of Orion is often seen, and one can sometimes watch shooting stars overhead as meteoroids enter the atmosphere from outer space.

In the early days after acquiring the property John Stott would reach The Hookses by means of the night sleeper train from Paddington to Haverfordwest, and then take a local taxi for the last 12 miles.

When the night sleeper service was discontinued, and long before the M4 motorway was built, John, with his secretary Frances Whitehead and Gwen Packer, would drive down to The Hookses. Gwen Packer, or 'Packie' as she was known, was the housekeeper at the Rectory in London.

She had lost her fiancé in the First World War and never married, and in the early days she would accompany John and Frances to The Hookses as their chaperone. They would leave at 5.00am, driving through the Cotswolds and stopping for breakfast at Ross-on-Wye, before motoring down the Welsh valleys onto the A40, a journey of eight hours which now takes half the time on the M4 motorway.

From the late 1970s onwards it often fell to John Stott's study assistants to drive him and Frances to The Hookses. Journeys were usually in the early morning, and sometimes driver and passenger would share a time of prayer and reading of scripture as they drove. One study assistant, Toby Howarth, recalls how John Stott found the long drive tedious and the inactivity

unwelcome, and on one occasion they both sang along to some old Fred Astaire songs. He also divulged that if John was driving and Frances was in the car, she might cast a glance at the speedometer remarking that maybe he was driving a little too fast. He would respond that if you looked at the needle on the gauge from the passenger's seat angle it appeared faster than if you looked at it straight on from the driver's seat!

Occasionally, journeys to The Hookses meant driving through

the middle of the day, and when that happened the car would be stopped in a layby so that John could stretch out on the verge by the roadside for a nap. He was able to fall asleep instantly and, exactly half-an-hour later, wake

Arriving on Skomer, 1984

Almighty and everlasting God,
Creator and Sustainer of the
universe, I worship you.
Lord Jesus Christ, Saviour and
Lord of the world, I worship
you.
Holy Spirit, Sanctifier of the
people of God, I worship you.
Glory be to the Father, and to the
Son and to the Holy Spirit
As it was in the beginning is now
and ever shall be, world without
end, Amen.
Lord Jesus Christ, I pray that this
day I may take up my cross and
follow you.
Holy Spirit, I pray that this day
your fruit will ripen in my life:
love, joy, peace, patience,
kindness, goodness, faithfulness,
gentleness and self-control.
Holy, blessed and glorious Trinity,
three persons in one God, have
mercy upon me. Amen

refreshed. On one occasion, this occurred to the astonished amusement of Mrs Evelyn Egtvedt who was being taken to see The Hookses. Her husband Clairmont Egtvedt had worked for the *Boeing* aircraft corporation as a draftsman and mechanical engineer in 1917 and rose to become Company President and acting Chairman of the board after William Boeing resigned in 1934. It was under his direction that the *Boeing Airplane Corporation* built the Clipper, the Stratoliner, the Flying Fortress and the Superfortress. He retired from *Boeing* in 1966, and died in 1975. His widow, Evelyn, had come to know John Stott in the United States through the Langham Foundation and had been a faithful supporter. On this occasion John Stott was delighted to be able to take her to visit The Hookses, where together they named 'The Lady Evelyn Stairway' that had been created above the waterfall.

Days at The Hookses with John Stott were strictly ordered but great fun. In his Hermitage a few steps away from the main house he would wake early and listen to the BBC World Service, and spend time in personal devotions and prayer which included the Trinitarian prayer that he used every morning (see left hand panel).

JRWS and Evelyn naming the steps

At 8.00am he would come up to the main house for breakfast. Never late, in the early days our young boys would sit by the window to wait and wave to him as he approached. Then back to his study for the morning and, depending on how his preparation was going, he might join his other guests for a small lunch. Then it was horizontal half hour (HHH) time or, as he was getting older,

Frances

JRWS, Matthew and John Smith

horizontal (w)hole hour. Following that, a time of 'do-it-yourself' or bird watching. It was usually possible to persuade him once or twice during the week – not that he needed much persuasion – to spend an hour or two on the Gann Estuary, one of his favourite bird-watching sites, just a couple of miles from The Hookses. Then it was back for a tea and more work until supper, when he would join his guests for a meal in the main house.

During meals, he would often come up with amusing jokes or stories, and liked the one about the two schoolboys who hated each other. After they grew up, one became an admiral and the other a bishop. Forty years later they met on the railway station, both in full dress, with instant recognition. The bishop was now overweight but he turned to the admiral and said, "Porter, will you take my bags to the train!" to which the admiral replied, "Madam, in your condition I wouldn't advise travelling anywhere!"

He was not usually involved in the cooking but insisted on doing the washing up, although on one occasion, walking back across the airfield one Sunday morning after church, he spied some mushrooms which were collected and made into mushroom soup, reciting over the pot as it was being stirred, "There's death in the pot!" Fortunately he was able to identify mushrooms correctly and death was avoided. After reading Ron Sider's book *Rich Christians in an Age of Hunger* he decided he would refuse second helpings, and continued to quietly demonstrate that he would "live simply that others may simply live." However, at the end of a meal when asked how it was, he would answer that it was fine but the last mouthful was a little bit bitter, indicating that he would like one piece of chocolate just to finish it off. So he was delighted one day to find a package in the fuel shed that would not fit through the letter box. It had been sent some weeks previously by Rosemary Bird, and in reply he wrote:

Cory and I went into the fuel shed yesterday afternoon to check the oil and what do you think we found? Two large slabs of chocolate from you. The postmark was December but because the parcels were too thick to go through the letterbox the postman left them in the fuel shed. The choccy is untouched by human hand and unnibbled by mousey teeth! So thank you very much. I've handed the chocolate to Cory so that he takes responsibility to do the distribution especially when bitter dessert needs to be compensated.

After supper, as coffee was served, Saki was often on the agenda. Read in the early days by the glow of soft oil lamps or later by gas lamps, the group would gather in the small sitting room and John would begin to read one of his favourite stories.

John had been introduced to Saki at Rugby, and the book from which he used to read has his signature in it with the date December 1939. Saki was the pen name of Hector Hugh Munro who died in the First World War at the age of 46. He was a British writer whose witty, mischievous and sometimes macabre stories satirise Edwardian society and culture. Brought up by maiden aunts after his mother's death, they feature in many of his stories.

The Lumber Room is about a small boy, Nicholas, who was not believed when he stated that there was a frog in his bread-and-milk. He had put it there himself, so he felt entitled to know something about it.

The sin of taking a frog from the garden and putting it into a bowl of bread-and-milk was enlarged on at great length, but the fact that stood out clearest in the whole affair, as it presented itself to the mind of Nicholas, was that the older, wiser, and better people had been proved to be profoundly in error in matters about which they had expressed the utmost assurance. "You said there could not possibly be a frog in my bread-and-milk, and there was a frog in my bread-and-milk," he repeatedly affirmed, with the insistence of a skilled tactician who does not intend to shift from favourable ground.

But *The Storyteller* was always John's favourite. It was a tale about a bachelor who was sharing the same railway carriage as an aunt and three of her charges. The aunt did not have a good reputation as a story teller and the bachelor suggested that he could tell the children a story, a suggestion with which they were delighted. It was about a young girl, Bertha, who was 'horribly good' – two words which, taken together, caught the children's immediate attention. Because of her goodness, Bertha was allowed to walk in the Royal garden, wearing the three medals she had been given for obedience, punctuality and good behaviour. This was a great privilege, until one day a wolf came prowling into the park, with "a black tongue and pale grey eyes that gleamed with unspeakable ferocity." He was looking for a little piglet, of which there were many in the Royal Park. But he ended up locating Bertha in the midst of a scented myrtle bush after hearing her medals clink together, and he devoured her to the last morsel.

It was a story which the children felt had a beautiful ending! However, the aunt disagreed, thinking it was a most improper story to tell to young children, undermining years of careful teaching. "At any rate" said the bachelor, "I kept them quiet for ten minutes, which was more than you were able to do," reflecting to himself that "for the next six months or so those children will assail her in public with demands for an improper story!"

Although John had recounted the tale countless times, he was never tired of reading it, usually with tears of laughter running down his face.

Whenever John was at The Hookses, the local birdlife was a continuing preoccupation. When studying at his desk in the Hermitage, a pair of binoculars would be ready on the desk beside him and in the early days, he persuaded friends to help him construct hides from which he could watch the birds more closely. The first hide was built with friends on the little headland at the end of the valley using old corrugated iron dragged from the debris on the airfield, covered in turf.

Hide by lesser blacked backed gulls, 1959

Hide at Hooper's Point, 1968

Hide at Buzzards' nest, Hooper's Point, 1968

From time to time, rare birds were spotted. One American visitor saw a black-winged stilt in Dale Castle meadow and entered the sighting in the visitors' book, adding the comment, "very rare in UK." On the following page, another visitor, not to be outdone, invented a new species and wrote, "Saw a brown sea owl at Dale Fort – very rare in UK"!

On one occasion Dick Bird came in one day proudly announcing he had seen a hoopoe on the Gann Estuary – a distinctive bird that was very familiar to him from his days in the Middle East. John was unimpressed until John Barrett, the local wildlife expert, confirmed that one had been seen in the area. Dick's ornithological reputation with John rose considerably after

that. In his book *People my Teachers* John writes that after a visit to Lystra in the footsteps of the Apostle Paul, he saw a pair of hoopoes and went on to say, "I shall always associate Lystra with hoopoes." I think my father-in-law thereafter always associated hoopoes with the Gann Estuary!

On one visit to Skomer with John Stott, two guillemots were seen in the air and it was difficult to decide whether they were fighting or mating. So the expert was asked, and the lifelong bachelor replied laconically that he understood there was not much difference between the two! On that trip he put his hand down a hole and pulled out a Manx shearwater. Those with him at the time were unaware that he had performed this manoeuvre several times in the past and on

one occasion, when he did it for Dick Lucas and friends, he was seen by the warden of Skomer and given a severe reprimand.

At John Stott's funeral service in All Souls Langham Place in 2011, Judge David Turner, a great friend of John's and one of the churchwardens at All Souls, told the story of how he arrived one day at the vestry for a meeting, adding that he had been dive-bombed by a seagull on the way from Oxford Circus. He was dabbing at his suit, and came in muttering "Wretched seagull...." John was, to say the least, unsympathetic!

A herring gull, a black-headed gull it may have been – a mere seagull it was not! Dear brother, you have been judged for your ignorance!

Guillemots

In 1950 John Stott moved into All Souls Rectory at 12 Weymouth Street, a six-storey Georgian house which was far too big for an unmarried Rector. So he asked the Church Council for their agreement to offer accommodation to curates and three or four other single men who were church members – so it was that his first curate John Collins moved in to be looked after by 'Packie', the housekeeper, and a cook.

Others stayed at the Rectory from time to time including one Canadian visitor who chided John for always reading *The Times*. "You should read *The Guardian* – it's a much better paper. Look, it's even got a picture of black-headed gull flying past a lighthouse!" John looked up from his *Times*, took the *Guardian* and glanced at the picture. "Actually," he said quietly, "it's an immature kittiwake!"

Dr Monty Barker stayed once and recalls his experience:

Two adult herring gulls and an immature gull, 1962

I had the privilege of staying with him on one occasion in the Rectory, colloquially known as the 'Stottery'. I was in a room at the top of the house, and breakfast was at the bottom of the house. One had to go back to the top after breakfast to clean one's teeth. It was very different from my Scottish background. The breakfast was sumptuous, whereas I was used to porridge! Everyone read the paper at table; in my home you never read in the company of others – meals were times for conversation. John asked, as I came down for breakfast, "Would you like a newspaper?" I said, "No thank you," but he still opened his and started reading it. After breakfast, we went into the drawing room and knelt down for prayers against the settee with its silk brocade and prayed together. It was quite an experience. A different world – and yet he was a man who had the most profound influence on my life.

John Collins described John Stott in his younger days as, "The most eligible Christian bachelor in London," and says that he

JRWS on cliffs, 1950s

of Frances Whitehead, *John Stott's Right Hand*, John Yates, one of John Stott's study assistants, reflected on the relationship between John and Frances, describing it as a deep mutual affection.

Both had a very clear sense of vocation. John's was to serve Christ's church through his ministry of writing, preaching and encouraging younger leaders. Frances' was to serve Christ's church through serving John, by making him more efficient and more effective. While deeply intertwined there was never an unhealthy co-dependency or a lobbying for something more in their relationship. There was a sense of joy in standing alongside each other and serving together.

suffered a little from the ladies. In the early days at All Souls Church one lady sat under the pulpit week after week as John was preaching and then moved up into the gallery above the pulpit, and many of John's friends were afraid that she would jump into the pulpit as he was preaching. Another was upset about his lack of willingness openly to confess his love for her. So as he stood greeting all the parishioners one by one at the door, she

bolted in and began to hit him on the shins with her umbrella – the people standing in line to greet the Rector were shocked. The victim jumped around a little, and then a couple of people took the woman away. He tried to remain calm as the lady in question was escorted away, but always behaved kindly to the individual making the fracas.

Many wondered if he and Frances would ever marry, and in Julia Cameron's biography

Mark Labberton, another study assistant, added that:

John was able to do what he did because Frances was able to do what she did. A joint calling and one which needed the driven and focused attention of each of them. Frances gave him much of the personal advantage of being married without being married.

With the Swannell's grandchildren, 1992

With Kwame Aboagye-Mensah, about 1984

With Jonathan and Andy Cranston and John Yates, 1997

With Sally Scott, 1992

He goes on to say, "I don't know another human being who could have kept up with John."

While he never doubted his calling, and felt that his singleness allowed him great freedom to travel and preach, he did from time to time have those wistful moments of thinking about family life. He was very conscious of the fact that bachelorhood represented a costly element in his own discipleship. On one occasion at The Hookses, walking across the airfield hand in hand with our son Andy, then about two years old, he admitted to Rosemary Bird, Andy's grandmother, "I suddenly realised what I was missing by not having a family."

Always popular with children, John had many honorary sons and daughters, grandsons and granddaughters and even great-grandsons and great-granddaughters. He never talked down to them, and would sit with his three nieces on the cliffs, reading *Treasures of the Snow*, enjoying the story with its dramatic struggles in the alpine meadows and snowcapped mountains of Switzerland.

Over the years guests have been encouraged to write in the visitors' books at The Hookses. There have been six books from the first entry on 12th April 1955 to the present day, with over 10,000 entries, and if

in London it was more difficult to entertain, The Hookses provided an opportunity to do so. It was here, in his own home, with the help of Frances or other close friends who were staying at the time, that local people from Dale would be invited up for drinks or for a meal, and of course many close friends and other guests would come and stay. John would often join his guests for meals and other activities, but it was on the understanding that he would need to retreat for long periods to the Hermitage, or to his favourite spot on the edge of the cliffs, to read, write, pray, and prepare for the next sermon series at All Souls or on an international visit.

The comments in The Hookses' visitors' books are testimony not only to the owner's love of birds, but to the influence he had on others. Two of many such entries were:

At a beautiful spot called The Hookses
John Stott's written dozens of bookses
And when not crafting words
then he's off watching birds –
choughs, peregrines, gannets and rookses.

Another visitor wrote: "I appreciate bird watching much more this year."

There are entries from groups and individuals, some with more fanciful names

JRWS sailing at Dale with John Collins, 1950s

JRWS with a young Andy Cranston

than others: The Charladies' houseparty; the University and Colleges Christian Fellowship (UCCF) writers and painters group; the Evangelical Churches of Wales. School and church groups came, left and returned year after year. The Hookses was host to the 'first annual training conference for retired mothers-in-law,' as well as 'the vicars' honeymoon-spoiling party', and the more serious Veterinary Surgeons' Christian Fellowship. Also 'The Scripture knowledge

sharks', 'tired-out deacons' week', and the 'Potential Polish Pastors Prayerfully Preparing in Pembrokeshire' group.

Many of the entries are from the younger generation, demonstrating their love for Uncle John and The Hookses. A young Louisa Nunn wrote:

I like The Hookses
We like to be at The Hookses
Plenty to do at The Hookses

Plenty to see at The Hookses
For a small fee at The Hookses.

And her sister Lydia, some years later: "Best week of the year – every Hookses gets better."

One wrote, "Mega Ace Brilliant Absolutely Spiffing," and another entry reads, "A double joy to discover both The Hookses and Saki."

Other individual entries come not only from the UK but across the globe, with some

View across West Dale Bay from The Hookses

claiming, "45 years of visits." One young South Korean visitor wrote:

Thank you for letting me have a great time here. I would choose here if I had to choose any place in the UK.

A Romanian guest wrote:

Speechless – we have seen where the fingers of God are at work.

Cory Widmer, one of John Stott's study assistants, brought his parents across from the United States and they wrote:

Finally a dream come true and it's even better than we imagined.

Steve Andrews, who became Bishop of Algoma in Canada, during his last visit as John's study assistant in May 1986 wrote:

Oh Wonderful Hookses, one day we will return.

In 1960 The Evangelical Fellowship in the Anglican Communion had come into being and John Stott inaugurated a Welsh section of this body; in April 1964 the individual Welsh members of this group were invited to spend the day at The Hookses. Coming from all over Wales to John Stott's exposition, 70 people crammed into The Hookses. In later years the morning meetings took place in Dale Parish Church, but even then there was standing room only for late comers.

A Place for Writing

In 1948 John Stott was ordained by William Wand, the Bishop of London, and two years later he instituted John as Rector of All Souls, Langham Place, situated at the top of Regent Street in London. John found him a bit formidable, but one thing he did at the institution was to urge John to take time to read and write, and three years later invited John to write the Bishop of London's Lent book. It was published in January 1954 and entitled *Men with a Message*, with the purpose of encouraging Christian people to read the New Testament for themselves as an incentive to Bible reading and not as a substitute for it. He received £700 in royalties for this book, and it was this money that allowed him to buy The Hookses, which in

Barnacle Goose

Lesser Black Backed Gulls' eggs with florin, 1959

Male stonechat, The Hookses, 1964

turn became the place where most of his other books were written.

John Stott always seemed to manage to take with him to The Hookses whatever he needed to write, even in the days before computers and internet access. He would write his books out in longhand, which Frances Whitehead would type, initially on a typewriter but later on computer. In the 1980s she made herself computer-literate when she was well into her 50s. In the days before electricity was brought across the airfield to The Hookses, she used an electric generator for power. As Dr Monty Barker described in the first chapter of this book, the writings of John Stott usually came from sermons he had preached, but unlike the writings of Martyn Lloyd-Jones, which were typed unchanged from his preaching, the books John created went through his mind twice or even three times before they were written down, for the written word is different from the spoken word.

Your Confirmation was based on the preparation that John Stott had been accustomed to give each year to young people in the parish of All Souls, first as Curate and then as Rector. It was written mainly at The Hookses in the company of Dick Lucas and John Collins, both of whom had been enlisted to contribute to the series, but alas it was only John Stott who produced a manuscript, and on the back cover of *Your Confirmation* appeared advertisements for forthcoming books by RC Lucas and JTCB Collins, eagerly awaited by the Christian public. In the words of John Collins, "They are still waiting!"

Another of the early Hookses' books was *Basic Christianity*, seeking to explain and commend the facts of the New Testament to both mind and heart, and stressing the need for a personal response. Translated into 25 languages, it has now sold about 1.5 million copies around the world.

The Preachers Portrait was an expansion of lectures delivered in 1961 at Fuller Theological Seminary at Pasadena, California. It is a series of New Testament word studies, asking the question, "What is a preacher?" and answering that he is a steward of God's word. And then he goes on to the famous homely illustration for his American audience:

The Englishman's favourite breakfast dish is eggs and bacon. We will suppose that a certain householder issues his steward or housekeeper eggs and bacon, with the instructions to dispense them to the household for breakfast on four successive mornings. On Monday morning the steward threw them into the garbage can and gave them fish instead. That is contradiction, and his Master was angry. On Tuesday morning he gave them eggs only, but not bacon. That is subtraction, and his Master was again angry. On Wednesday morning he gave them eggs and bacon and sausages. That is addition, and his Master was still angry. But in the end, on Thursday morning, he gave them eggs and bacon – nothing else, nothing less, nothing more, and his Master was well pleased with him at last!

He goes on to say that the household of God urgently needs faithful stewards who will dispense to it systematically the whole word of God. Not the New Testament only but the Old as well; not the best known text only, but also the lesser-known; not just the passages which favour the preacher's particular prejudices, but those which do not!

In *I Believe in Preaching* he writes of his personal difficulty in the early days of his ministry of taking time to prepare, and how difficult it was for him, and indeed how stressful he found it, until he discovered the immense profit, through an address at one clerical conference, of the quiet day at least once a month. He goes on to say:

But the minimum would amount to this: every day at least one hour; every week one morning, afternoon or evening; every month a full day; every year a week. Set out like this, it sounds very little. Indeed, it is too little. Yet everybody who tries it is surprised to discover how much reading can be done with such a disciplined framework. It adds up to nearly 600 hours in the course of the year.

It revolutionised his own life and brought huge blessing to his life and ministry, and of course The Hookses became an integral part of this 'time apart.' He finished *I Believe in Preaching* in December 1980 at The Hookses and sent Frances, who was in London at the time, a two-word telegram reading 'tetelestai alleluia': It is finished, alleluia.

The Cross of Christ was his 'magnum opus' and it was the one book to feature by name on his gravestone. He completed it in 1985 and wrote from The Hookses in December, six months after my father-in-law's death, when he was with Rosemary (Bird) and Frances:

Your favourite mother-in-law, though occasionally wearing a wistful and faraway look, is wonderfully brave and we are all

JRWS at his desk, 2006

laughing lots, mostly about stale jokes! The Lord has given me a good week revising and polishing *The Cross of Christ*. I long to be enabled to at least begin to do justice to this magnificent theme. Frances is typing her fingers off. Steve [Andrews] is checking typescript and endnotes and compiling a Bibliography. Fauna [Andrews] is aiding and abetting, and your mother-in-law is presiding graciously over the whole scene.

He was alone at The Hookses in December 1987 when he wrote:

I have just returned from my travels in East Europe and Asia, full of admiration for the courage of Christians behind the Iron Curtain (especially in Romania), who refuse to be intimidated or dispirited by oppression, and I am deeply thankful

Steve and Fauna Andrews

In another letter from The Hookses he writes:

It has been marvellous to have these five weeks down here, with one still to go. I've been able to finish editing the book of Lausanne documents, to check the proofs of *The Bible Speaks Today* on 1 Timothy and Titus, and to read the first eight chapters of Timothy Dudley-Smith's biography, at his insistence, which take me up to Ordination. He has been quite astonishingly meticulous in his research and balanced in his presentation. I'm extremely fortunate to have him as a biographer.

In 1996 John Stott turned 75 and was at The Hookses working on his compilation of documents from the Lausanne movement. He wrote,

It is Spring migration time: down here two days ago, I heard the raucous call of the sandwich tern, looked up and saw them in West Dale Bay flying north to North Wales. Yesterday I heard the seven-whistle call of the whimbrel and there were nine flying north to breed in the Scottish highlands – marvellous.

for the outstanding quality of the emerging leadership of Third World churches, but also dismayed by the almost pathological tendencies of evangelicals to go on splintering and refusing to cooperate. A bitter-sweet experience. I'm down here alone this week, enduring a painful struggle. David Edwards (leading Church of England scholar and Church historian)

has written a manuscript entitled 'What is Essential for Evangelicals?' It is in reality a critical review of my 'published works'. He begins with flattery and continues with a devastating critique. First the butter, then the dagger! I'm crying to God for a special anointing of the Spirit of Truth that I may defend and commend our precious evangelical faith. Please pray for me!

Todd Shy
1988-1992

Nelson Gonzalez
1993-1996

John Yates
1996-1999

Corey Widmer
1999-2002

Matthew Smith
2002-2005

Tyler Wigg Stevenson
2005-2006

Chris Jones ("CJ")
2006-2007

Roy McCloughry
1977-1978

Tom Cooper
1978-1980

Mark Labberton
1980-1981

Steve Ingraham
1981-1982

Bob Wismer
1982-1984

Steve Andrews
1984-1986

Toby Howarth
1986-1988

Study assistants 1997-2007

Increasing years brought a certain physical frailty, although apart from a very brief spell off work following an operation to repair a hernia (which despite being a Cambridge man he allowed Oxford to host), he could claim in his early 70s, "I don't think I've had a day in bed for 40 years!"

John Stott could have made a lot of money from his writings. But after using the royalties from *Men with a Message* to purchase The Hookses, 95% of his royalties went to charitable trusts such as the Langham Trust or the Evangelical Literature Trust which were used to distribute books to pastors, theological teachers and students, and seminary libraries in the developing world, and he would encourage other authors to do the same.

After his appointment as Rector Emeritus in 1975, John Stott was able to spend more time writing and travelling but needed help with research and proof-reading, and so it was that the post of study assistant came into being. The Hookses was always an integral part of the study assistant's role and often the most enjoyable part. John, Frances and the current study assistant would often be alone at The Hookses, especially in the winter months, and the study assistant would help in various ways with John's writing, proof-reading or checking references.

The post of study assistant began with Roy McCloughry in 1977 and finished in 2007 with Chris Jones. A number were sons of friends who had known John Stott since childhood; others were recommended to him.

In his 2001 New Year letter John Stott writes:

It was Charles Simeon of Holy Trinity Church in Cambridge at the beginning of the nineteenth century who referred to himself and his two curates as "this happy triumvirate." So we have adopted it in reference to the indomitable Frances Whitehead, my current study assistant Cory Widmer and myself. We work well together and enjoy each other.

Cory Widmer's entry in the visitors' book at The Hookses in January 2000, when he and 'Uncle John' were working on the London Lectures for later that year, reads:

Ah! the monkish life at The Hookses, huddling in our room sheltered from the unrelenting wind!

Jonathan Cranston acted as a locum study assistant for two months in the summer of 2002 after Cory Widmer left and before

Matthew Smith arrived. He gave a resume of his role in an email to his friends:

I think my best bet is to start with the present! I am at the moment sitting at a desk in the Hermitage at The Hookses, Dale, Haverfordwest. For those of you who don't know what The Hookses is, it is the retreat cottage of John Stott. For those of you who don't know who he is then you're clearly not reading enough Christian literature. Enough said! My view out of the window is of the Irish Sea, if my geography is correct: birds, cliffs – truly wonderful.... I am working as a temporary study assistant for John Stott; temporary means until the university term starts again. My job description is indefinable. I have in the last two weeks done most things from reading books for him, running round most of London's Christian bookshops trying to find various books for him, entertaining people with names that can't be pronounced, acting as a bodyguard after church on Sunday, taking clothes to the dry cleaners, picking up prescriptions, sanding down and painting the chest of drawers, chauffeuring him about – and the list goes on! My biggest responsibility is probably cooking for him – I hear you laugh, well I'm not that bad – by that I mean he is still alive. Last night my talents provided bangers and very watery mash (too much milk!).... I think I must be going in a minute – put on my chef's hat and cook up a cocktail of culinary delights – beans on toast!

It was while Jonathan and John were clearing weeds from the stream that John tripped and fell badly injuring his leg on a large stone. Although not broken it did require an admission to hospital in Haverfordwest followed by three weeks of recuperation, and it was some months before he was allowed to fly again. It was during this period that *Why I Am a Christian* was written. Jonathan's entry in the visitors' book reads, "Certainly an eventful time!"

Other Authors

Many others have gone to The Hookses and found the peace and tranquillity to write. Timothy Dudley-Smith remembers the image, as night fell, of the twinkling lights of HMS Harrier, the shore-based Royal Naval Radar and Meteorological Training Station at Kete,

two miles to the south of Dale. To the imaginative eye, the single storey flat-roof buildings seemed to have a Middle Eastern look about them and were therefore known at The Hookses as Damascus. This provided the inspiration of the third verse of the poem that Timothy wrote as he lay awake on the night sleeper returning to London in 1959, and it can still be seen today, framed in the dining room at The Hookses. Ten years later, Neil Jackson added the penultimate verse (see page 66).

Revd Dr Alec Motyer was another visitor to The Hookses in the early days. He later became joint principal of Trinity College Bristol, and was the Old Testament editor of *The Bible Speaks Today* series and a respected Hebrew scholar. He reflected on his visits there with Dick Bird and John Stott in a letter written in 1995:

Every memory of Dickie Bird is a blessing. In those far off days at The Hookses we were all, of course, equals but there was one of our happy trio that was notably more equal than Dickie and I, so he and I – if Rosemary wasn't present – made common cause to keep

The Great One happy and make sure his meals were served on time. Dickie and I were self-appointed members, and JRWS chairman of the washing up committee. We had such fun. He (Dickie) was getting on with all sorts of mysteries of electron microscopy and I, for the most part, was ferreting around in Isaiah – though one year, probably 1969, I was working on Psalms for the revision of the New Bible Commentary. In 1970 we returned to college work in Bristol and it was the end of The Hookses invitations. I did not see Dickie again but look forward to Glory.

In 2007, Alec Motyer shared the platform at the Keswick Convention with John Stott for the last time. He wrote:

It is a fact. Never in the history of the Keswick Convention have two speakers enjoyed a combined age of 168 years! My elderly eyes were blind with tears as I watched my beloved friend make his slow way to the platform, marked his resolute stance at the lectern, and thanked God with the thousands present for the best evening meeting of

On the Gann Estuary, 1998

O happy times at Hookses! Long
    hours of leisured ease
On Pembroke's pastoral forehead
    caressed by wind and seas:
The black-backed and the herring gull
    soar swiftly o'er the bay;
The greater has the blacker back, the
    lesser's back is grey.

O happy days at Hookses! O days of
    sea and sky!
O peaceful paths of lost content! O
    steak and kidney pie!
O hours of exercise and toil with long
    and arduous climbs!
O hours of erudition with the
    crossword from *The Times*.

O happy nights at Hookses – for
    when the days decline
The lamps of little Eastern homes far
    from Damascus shine.
High in the vault of Hookses' sky the
    stars their vigil keep:
For us, in earth's diurnal course,
    eleven hours of sleep.

O happy stars at Hookses – Plough,
    Pleiades and Orion:
Beneath you lies a mound of turf and
    corrugated iron
In which, as on a slab nearby, the

birds dismember rabbits,
The Rector notes with all-seeing eye
    their predatory habits.

O happy climbs at Hookses, with
    baskets and with bait
We brave the crumbling sandstone to
    seal the lobster's fate.
The crafty old crustacean knows what
    the basket's for,
And grasps the bait from outside with
    armour-plated claw.

O happy times at Hookses, how fast
    the moments fly
To eat and idle, swim and sleep, and
    then to say goodbye.
So soon the last long lingering look,
    so soon the London train,
O may it bring me swift and soon to
    Hookses Vale again!

And in April 2001 Timothy Dudley-
Smith penned the following lines for John
Stott's 80th birthday:

O happy times at Hookses! How
    sweet the sight appears!
A scallop shell, a hermit's cell, for all
    but fifty years!
How sweet for feet, so fleet and neat,
    the 'Frances Whitehead' path;

How sweet the bright electric light,
    and how ensuite the bath.
O happy birds at Hookses! What
    eagle eyes remark,
The Grebes and Choughs, the Reeves
    and Ruffs, the Linnet and the
    Lark;
What zest expressed by ceaseless
    quest, in search of feathered fowl;
And, last and best, upon its nest, the
    long-sought Snowy Owl.

What halcyon days at Hookses!
    Delights that never end!
To stare with studious lookses at
    Ravens, Crows and Rookses,
And many a feathered friend.
As Frances Whitehead cookses
    beneath its friendly roofs,
To sit in sheltered nookses, or by its
    babbling brookses
And write us lots more bookses, while
    Corey reads the proofs.

O happy happy Hookses! The
    peaceful hours go by;
The days to write, the starry night, the
    sun the sea the sky:
And friends enough to wish you joy,
    as still you journey on;
With one accord we thank the Lord
    for eighty years of John!

happy times at Hookses!
Long hours of leisured ease
On Pembroke's pastoral forehead
Caressed by winds and seas:
The black-backed and the herring-gull
Soar swiftly o'er the bay;
(the greater has the blacker back,
The lesser's back is grey).

O happy days at Hookses!
O days of sea and sky!
O peaceful paths of lost content!
O steak-and-kidney pie!
O hours of exercise and toil
With long and arduous climbs!
O hours of erudition
With the crossword from *The Times!*

O happy nights at Hookses –
For when the days decline
The lamps of little Eastern homes
From far Damascus shine.
High in the vault of Hookses sky
The stars their vigil keep:
For us. in earth's diurnal course,
Eleven hours of sleep.

O happy stars at Hookses –
Plough. Pleiads. and Orion:
Beneath you lies a mound of turf
And corrugated iron:
In which. as on a slab nearby
The birds dismember rabbits
The Rector notes. with all seeing eye
Their predatory habits.

O happy climbs at Hookses!
With basket and with bait
We brave the crumbling sandstone
To seal the lobster's fate.
The crafty old crustacean
Knows what the basket's for
And grasps the bait from outside
With armour-plated claw.

O happy times at Hookses!
How fast the moments fly:
To eat and idle. swim and sleep –
And then to say goodbye.
So soon the last long lingering look.
So soon the London train!
O may it bring me swift and soon
To Hookses Vale again!

Timothy Dudley-Smith   June 1959

Neil Jackson (v.5)   Jan. 1969

the week. All the accustomed clarity of thoughts and presentation and, as ever, total devotion and faithfulness to the word of God. The same two antiquarians could have been seen eating together on the Monday evening, and breakfasting together on Tuesday and Wednesday mornings. This was joy indeed. My mind went back 50 years to the first time I sat beside John – in the library at Lambeth Palace whither we had been summoned to register a protest at the way the revision of Canon Law in the Church of England was then proceeding. He did not know me then and I was too in awe to speak to him. But rich memories came from the 1960s when he used to invite me annually as a neighbouring vicar to share a study week at The Hookses. That was when, for me, admiration blossomed into a loving friendship which the years, in spite of tragic infrequency of meeting, have served to increase. John was taken by surprise, and I think a bit embarrassed, that both on meeting and parting (at Keswick) I kissed him on forehead or hand. But that is what 1 Thessalonians 5v26 directs – even if his commentary says it should be interpreted as a 'culturally appropriate gesture'. Never mind culture. How else should I greet one I love and revere in equal measure? Keswick came and went, and the goodness of our Lord Jesus saw both him and me through its demands. We both sang our swan songs to that huge gathering, and now we both turn, to what Charles Simeon described as, "running with all our might now that the winning post is in sight." Running! My Zimmer frame trails far behind his, I fear, but I long with all my heart to be identified, however feebly, with his legacy. To know, love, read, study and proclaim the Word of God as long as the Lord gives life and his grace gives strength.

JOHN STOTT'S EARTHLY RESTING PLACE

CHRIS WRIGHT

The swallows and martins twittered over our heads, the cattle grazed contentedly a few yards away, and the wind whipped in off nearby West Dale Bay as we gently lowered the casket of John Stott's ashes into a small grave in the corner of the cemetery in Dale, on the very tip of south-west Wales.

It was John's wish that, after the funeral service at All Souls Church and cremation in London, his ashes should be buried in Dale. So it was that on Sunday 4th September 2011, a service of thanksgiving was held in the village church of St James the Great.

It had been a sunny morning but, as is common on this exposed coast, we moved from summer into autumn during lunchtime, as steep black clouds raced in from the sea with torrential rain. So people crowded into the little church from 2.15pm onwards, shaking out coats and umbrellas. There is nothing like the rain, though, to stimulate cheerful British conversation, as the church eventually filled to capacity with about eighty people gathered. Some were members of the congregations from the village churches of Dale, St Brides and Marloes, with whom John

regularly worshipped when staying at The Hookses. Some were pastors from the wider region: members of the informal group of Pembrokeshire pastors that meets twice a year at The Hookses for a day – started by John Stott and now carried on by myself when I go down there.

But the local community had come along too. There was Sharon, the wife of the farmer who owns the sheep on the land surrounding The Hookses. There was Keith, the village plumber who has serviced the boilers at The Hookses for years (and still does), who later stood alone with head bowed by the graveside paying his respects. There was Sheila, the lady who comes up once a week to check the place between visitors. There was Mrs Reynolds, whose husband did some of the first building work for John in the 1950s. And of course, there was Caroline Bowerman, John's niece, with her daughter Emily, son John and his girlfriend Michelle, for whom this was a final family farewell to their 'Uncle Johnnie.' Frances Whitehead was there too of course, with Matthew Smith, one of that apostolic band of study assistants who, one after

Dale Church interior

another, had formed 'the happy triumvirate' with John and Frances over many years of study and writing at The Hookses. David Gallagher, the architect who designed the wonderful upgrading and extension of the property over the past ten years, was there. And still others had come from further afield, including David and Christina Manohar from India, Langham scholars currently living in Cheltenham.

At 3.00 pm the service began, led by Revd Bill Lewis, a retired vicar from Milford Haven, one of John's oldest friends in the region. We followed the Anglican Order of Evening Prayer of the Church in Wales, including its beautiful canticles and prayers. We made the church resound with Christ-centred hymns sung to great Welsh melodies: 'Jesu, Lover of My Soul'; 'How Sweet the Name of Jesus Sounds'; and 'O the Deep, Deep Love of Jesus' – to the tunes Aberystwyth, Lloyd, and Ebenezer. Warm words of thanksgiving were brought, first by Revd Will Strange, Chair of the Evangelical Fellowship of the Church in Wales, which John had been instrumental in founding (at The Hookses!) in 1967, and then by Revd Rob James, representing the Evangelical Alliance of Wales. But then Bill Lewis opened it up for anyone to stand up and speak. Some rich Welsh accents spoke warmly of the affection they had for John. Mary, a retired schoolteacher from Milford Haven, told how John had allowed her to bring groups of teenagers to The Hookses regularly for camps, and some of them had come to faith in Christ there. The Revd Peter Davies, a former vicar of Dale, marvelled that John had thrown himself so fully into supporting the life of the local churches every time he came to Wales. One elderly gentleman delighted in telling us how John always looked him directly in the eye every time they spoke after church.

The prayer time, too, Bill opened up to all the congregation, and thanksgiving echoed around the pews – for John's love for the community, for the books he had written in that very place, for making The Hookses so available to others, for the gospel he had preached and lived.

Dale Church

I preached the sermon, as John had requested. I referred (as I did at All Souls) to John's daily prayer to each person of the Holy Trinity, asking, when he addressed the Holy Spirit, that the fruit of the Spirit should be seen in his own life. It is not hard to see how richly God answered John's daily prayer, in a life that was in so many ways simply like that of Jesus. But, I pointed out, we should not think that it was all the nice things about John that made him 'a true Christian gentleman.' It was the other way about. It was only because he had invited Christ into his life as a boy, and in that way had taken the first step in the Christian life, that God had been able to shape his character so fully through the Spirit of Christ within him. I knew John would have wanted the gospel to be preached with the local community gathered together, and so I read a short extract from his book *Why I Am a Christian*, describing how he accepted Christ as Saviour, to turn his estrangement into reconciliation and his defeat into victory, and I concluded by urging all present to follow John in that response to Jesus.

When the service in church was at an end, we opened the church door to the joyful discovery that the rain had blown over; there was still a stiff breeze, but blue skies could be seen moving in from the west. Bill and I led a procession from the church, myself carrying the casket with John's ashes, around the country lane to the little village cemetery. John had selected the spot where he wanted to be buried – close to the far wall that separates the cemetery from the cow-field on the other side, beside the grave of an old friend he knew in the village. When family and friends had gathered around closely in the wet grass, Bill prayed a final prayer of thanksgiving and committal, as I lowered the casket into the small grave. Silence reigned for some moments, apart from the birdsong and the grazing cattle nearby. Then people began to move around. Some wept and hugged, or just paid their respects at the tiny grave, and went on chatting until Paul the local gravedigger (a friendly man who told me his own father had died just the previous week, so it was an emotional time for him too) asked us if we would care to let him get on with filling in the grave, since he had another one to attend to later.

John had asked that a gravestone would eventually be placed at the spot, carved out of Welsh slate, with the words borrowed from Charles Simeon's memorial in Cambridge:

Buried here are the ashes of
JOHN R. W. STOTT
1921 – 2011
Rector of All Souls Church,
Langham Place, London 1950–1975
Rector Emeritus 1975–2011
Who resolved
Both as the ground of his salvation
And as the subject of his ministry
To know nothing except
JESUS CHRIST
And him crucified
(1 Corinthians 2:2)

We returned then, as the sun began to break through the clouds, to the church, where there were tea and biscuits waiting for us, and yet more anecdotes to be shared as we stood around. Tears glistened in the eyes of some of the burly men who told me how proud and pleased they were that John Stott – whose worldwide ministry they had some inkling of – had chosen to honour their village as his final resting place on earth. They seemed to feel that, in coming back to Dale, he had come home. Maybe in some ways he had. At any rate, the place seems utterly fitting for a man who, like Moses, was one of the greatest leaders God has given to his people, and yet one of the humblest men on earth. I can think of no more appropriate place for his earthly memorial than that small corner of a tiny village cemetery in the midst of lush green fields, on the very edge of the land he loved, surrounded by birds and cattle, with ivy, wild flowers and brambles climbing over the ancient red sandstone walls on either side, and the salty wind blowing in off the ocean.

RECTOR OF ALL SOULS CHURCH LANGHAM PLACE LONDON 1950-1975

BURIED HERE
ARE THE ASHES OF

JOHN
ROBERT WALMSLEY
STOTT
1921-2011

AND AS RECTOR EMERITUS 1975-2011

WHO RESOLVED
BOTH AS THE GROUND OF HIS SALVATION
AND AS THE SUBJECT OF HIS MINISTRY
TO KNOW NOTHING EXCEPT
JESUS CHRIST
AND HIM CRUCIFIED
1 CORINTHIANS 2:2

'The Cross of Christ' and many other books
were written at his retreat, The Hookses, Dale

Pembrokeshire cliffs

74

John Stott had an on-going vision for The Hookses to continue to be used to the best advantage as a Christian retreat centre. The exposure and nature of the site, environmental sensitivity and limitations on the services make its care complex. Many small donations and legacies have been used over the years for its upkeep and improvement and any gifts, however large or small, are welcome.

The situation of The Hookses in the Pembrokeshire National Park limits development on the site, though some further sensitive additions may still be feasible if suitable significant funds were available. The addition of a further multi-purpose meeting room or small chapel might be possible subject to planning permission. This would offer greater flexibility for more varied retreat weeks and add to The Hookses for current and future generations, but this would require further exploration and extensive investment.

The **Langham Partnership** is a global fellowship working in pursuit of the vision entrusted to its founder, John Stott, to strengthen the growth of the church in the majority world, in mission, maturity and Christlikeness, through raising the standards of biblical preaching and teaching, providing evangelical books, and strengthening theological education in seminaries. The name 'Langham' comes from All Souls Church, Langham Place, in London UK where John Stott ministered for nearly 60 years. For further information and donations please visit or contact:

www.langham.org

Any royalties from this book will be shared between The Langham Partnership (Hookses account) and the Oxford Centre for Mission Studies.

The **Oxford Centre for Mission Studies** was founded in 1983 and since then, 120 Christian leaders from around the world have completed their doctorates and all but two have returned to their home countries. In 2008 John Stott wrote,

The Oxford Centre for Mission Studies is an organisation with which I have been involved since its inception in 1983, and I have watched its development with great satisfaction. It is the conviction of OCMS, which I share, that during this century many of the influential leaders in the church will come from the global south. The on-going work of OCMS in preparing many of them for leadership, through its postgraduate and research programmes, will be a key part in this process.

For further information and donations please visit: *www.ocms.ac.uk*

A rainbow over The Hookses

Other Books by David Cranston available from WORDS BY DESIGN and Regnum Books

John Radcliffe and his Legacy to Oxford

David Cranston

978-1-909075-18-4 / 86pp / hb

"Dr Cranston has written a biography, as intriguing as it is scholarly, of one of Oxford's most remarkable benefactors. The incalculable benefits to science, medicine and architecture of Dr Radcliffe's largesse 300 years ago live on to this day and are an eloquent testimony to the vital contribution made by visionary philanthropy to the mission of a university: education, scholarship, research and the public good."

Sir Ivor Crewe, The Master, University College

I am delighted as a physician to commend a book written by a surgeon about a physician.

Sir Roger Bannister CH

On Eagles' Wings

David Cranston

978-1-908355-46-1 / 91pp / pb

This book introduces the concept of mentoring, looks at historical and biblical models and then gives examples of being mentored and acting as a mentor in the church and in the workplace.

"David Cranston writes unashamedly as a Christian for whom no account of mentoring would be complete without placing it in the biggest context of all – that of the relationship between humans and God."

Prof John Lennox, University of Oxford

"This gem of a book emerges from a lifetime's reflection on the vital, but neglected topic of mentoring."

Rev Richard Cunningham, UCCF

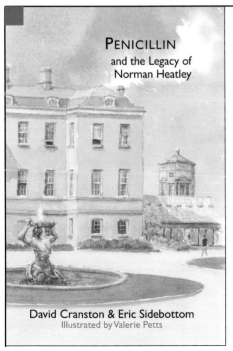

Penicillin and the Legacy of Norman Heatley

David Cranston and Eric Sidebottom

978-1-909075-46-7 / 100pp / hb

"At last, a biography of the crucial member of the Oxford research team that gave the world penicillin."

Professor Max Blythe, Green Templeton College

"...the most human and humble person you could ever imagine, and his work on the development of penicillin will last for ever."

Paul N. Rimmer, Vicar of Marston, 1959-90

"It is remarkable that while his colleagues were receiving the world's acclaim for the development of penicillin, the crucial contribution of Norman Heatley was largely forgotten. What is equally remarkable is that, in subsequent years, he never expressed even a hint of disappointment or envy at his exclusion."

Sir James Gowans, Fellow of the Royal Society

William Osler and his Legacy to Medicine

David Cranston

978-1-909075-48-1 / 132pp / hb

"William Osler was one of the founding fathers of the Johns Hopkins Hospital. David Cranston's biography will help to keep his name alive, and in these days of increasing technological advance remind all those involved in health care that humanity must remain central, and that, in Osler's own words 'the patient who has the disease is more important than the disease that has the patient'."

Prof Robert Montgomery, Formerly Director of the Comprehensive Transplant Center, The Johns Hopkins Hospital

A delightful introduction to *The Hookses* – a place of rest and renewal for many and a place for retreat, as well as a base for writing, for John Stott, perhaps the most outstanding evangelical statesman in the second half of the twentieth century – this enchanting book traces the history of the purchase and use of this former farmhouse in West Wales and its use by one of the great evangelical preachers and writers of the last generation.

Lindsay Brown, former General Secretary of IFES 1991-2007, International Director of the Lausanne Movement 2008-2016

What was the secret behind John Stott's insightful and prolific biblical and pertinent writing? Piety and prayer, surely! But also beloved people and a lovely place. This book is a vivid testimony as to how lasting friendships and a silent retreat in a secluded corner of creation served as fertile ground for 'Uncle John's' teaching and writing ministry and also provides an inspiration for its readers to embark on similarly fruitful paths.

Ruth Padilla DeBorst, Director of the Comunidad de Estudios Teológicos Interdisciplinarios (CETI) and Networking Team Coordinator of the International Fellowship for Mission as Transformation (INFEMIT)

If Evangelicals celebrated 'holy sites', an old farm on the south west coast of Wales, The Hookses, John Stott's country home, would certainly be regarded as such a place. My good friend, David Cranston, provides us with a wonderful tour of this pastoral setting where John Stott would retreat to rest, pray, and study. It was also at The Hookses that John Stott wrote 51 books, and hundreds of sermons that continue to be read and heard in London and around the world. John Stott did his preparatory work at The Hookses for writing the historic Lausanne Covenant, and it was there that his friend and successor, Chris Wright, wrote the Cape Town Commitment in 2010. This book is a treasure house in every sense of the word!

S. Douglas Birdsall, Honorary Chair, The Lausanne Movement

David Cranston, a close friend of John Stott, takes us to The Hookses, John's Pembrokeshire retreat, with fascinating stories and pictures. It is an entrancing book, a real treasure for all those influenced by John Stott.

Michael Green, Senior Research Fellow, Wycliffe Hall Oxford

One of the many pioneering initiatives John Stott supported was the Oxford Centre for Mission Studies. At OCMS we are passionate about understanding mission in context, for context always shapes the way God's truth is revealed and understood. That's why this beautiful journey around The Hookses is worth enjoying. David Cranston takes us into the context from which John Stott brought such biblical riches to the world. If silence and solitude are essential spiritual disciplines for those who would journey deep into the heart of God, then The Hookses provided John Stott with such a space.

Paul Bendor-Samuel, Executive Director Oxford Centre for Mission Studies, Sundo Kim Research Tutor in Global Mission